This Thing Called
MARKETING

This Thing Called

MARKETING

Jonathan Lezon

University of Arkansas—Fayetteville

cognella®

SAN DIEGO

Bassim Hamadeh, CEO and Publisher
Angela Schultz, Senior Field Acquisitions Editor
Michelle Piehl, Senior Project Editor
Christian Berk, Associate Production Editor
Emely Villavicencio, Senior Graphic Designer
Stephanie Kohl, Licensing Coordinator
Natalie Piccotti, Director of Marketing
Kassie Graves, Vice President of Editorial
Jamie Giganti, Director of Academic Publishing

3970 Sorrento Valley Blvd., Ste. 500, San Diego, CA 92121

CONTENTS

INTRODUCTION

When I decided to write a college-level marketing textbook, I honestly had no idea how to do it. Let's just get that out of the way early. However, I did know that I wanted to do it. I knew that it was going to take a lot of time. And I knew that, above all, it was going to take a commitment to the publisher once I agreed to embark on this journey. I wanted to write an honest work that talks to you, the reader, exactly how I talk in real life.

I had no idea where to start or what to say because I'd never written a book, never written a novel, or even an article. Nothing. Nada.

I am happy with the way it turned out due to a lot of help that I've received along the way by friends, colleagues, family, and students. The one thing I want you to understand before reading this book is that every page is devoted to being simple, deliberate, and dedicated to the integrity of marketing.

Most of all, I'm not spending a lot of time on a bunch of theory. I am providing my work experience—referenced by doing, failing (A LOT), and failing again. You will fail in your career. You will have people who have assumed a position of power that make you scratch your head, and you will have managers who just don't like you. Does that sound harsh? It is the world of business, but it is ALL a learning experience. Keep your head high, and always laugh and love. And remember, it is the business world. Guess what? You will also have people who inspire you, people you inspire, and you affect them in very positive ways during your career.

For over 30 years, I worked mainly in the consumer electronics realm and am now a partner in a business that I thoroughly enjoy. So, with that in mind, I'm going to be talking to you about real-life experiences: what I've gleaned from my experiences working with many companies, products, buyers, colleagues, and various other individuals and entities along the way. I believe we've captured a great introductory book to help you understand as clearly as possible what is involved with marketing. I hope you think so, too.

So, with that said, I'd like to introduce you to *This Thing Called Marketing*, an introduction to marketing focused on giving college students a glimpse into the field of marketing, the intricacies within the differing levels of acumen that are involved in producing effective marketing communications, campaigns, and programs. There are a multitude of facets to the exciting environment professionals are involved in surrounding marketing. This book is designed to break down the very complicated field of marketing and discuss it in sections, again with an introductory point of view. It has been written for college students who are new to the concept of marketing and want to understand the elements of the process.

The overarching goal of this work is to help students understand the complexity of marketing without making it complex. I will be talking to you throughout this work as if I was sitting next to you in my office. I believe that is the way to communicate—succinctly, to the point, and in layman's terms.

I am a firm believer in saying exactly what you mean and meaning what you say.

You've seen and heard people in your life who talk in circles, confounding with syllables, adjectives, and run-on sentences that make it appear that he or she is trying to show you how smart they are. It's unnecessary and should be avoided at all cost.

When you are professionals in marketing, sales, finance, accounting, operations, information systems, or whatever role you pursue in your career, keep it simple—always. As you grow in your career and progress up the echelon of command in organizations, you will realize that senior managers don't have time to hear someone speak just to hear themselves speak. They want to understand your position on a certain topic, why you have the position, and what steps you're going to take to implement your strategy. Period. By the way, as you become that senior manager, you're going to feel the same way. I like the Elon Musk approach to language and meetings: if you need a meeting, meet; and if you don't, don't.

It's that simple, it truly is. Don't make marketing (or any aspect of your life) complicated. Why would you do that? Because quite honestly, marketing really isn't complex if viewed and studied in its differing elements. It's a lot of fun. There's a lot of creativity involved and a lot of great marketing minds that help create programs designed to help their organizations succeed in business. These chapters you're about to read all have a key idea and key terms that will be further broken down as the flow of the chapter ensues.

Please join me as I discuss the many areas of marketing that are imperative to an organization's success. It's fun, collaborative, and exciting, and I'm happy that you've decided to join me as we begin the discussion of an introduction to marketing.

CHAPTER 1

DEFINING MARKETING

Marketing is pervasive: it's all around us. It's seen everywhere we go and involved in everything we do, and we are exposed to marketing in its many different forms.

Have you ever walked through an airport and noticed how many times between the ticket counter and gate that you're bombarded with messaging and advertising about food, local businesses, causes, electronics products, massages, alcohol? There are even Johnston & Murphy shoe outlets in airports and Louis Vuitton bags that can be purchased. There are literally thousands of messages aimed at you and your disposable income before you even sit down at your gate to board your plane. You are a captive audience; you are in a space where you're waiting and spending time. And guess what? Marketers know it. Because you're a captive audience, companies invariably charge you higher prices because they know you've got to be there anyway.

Should a liter of water at an airport *really* cost almost $5.00? It's insane, isn't it? You know why it costs that much? Again, you're a captive audience. You have to wait to buy water once you've passed through security. This is another aspect of marketing that involves place and time, which we will cover later. You and I are bombarded by marketing messages everywhere, and it is never going to stop. Why? Because we are all selling to someone or being sold to all day, every day. In some sense, we are all selling. It doesn't have to be in a formal setting or in a boardroom. It can be as simple as asking your spouse for some time out with the guys. We sell others about our brand, our persuasion, our beliefs, our time, our knowledge, even our favorite football team (go Vols!).

Do you believe me? It's true.

FIGURE 1.1. Hong Kong Airport Store

An example of a typical airport convenience store.

What is this Thing Called Marketing?

Marketing is a key function in any organization and is a very deliberate set of processes designed to improve a company's position within their industry. Companies use the creativity and expertise of individuals within the organization to set marketing parameters in place to improve their brand recognition. What does that mean? It means that everyone involved in the process (the company, you, me) wants to improve how they are viewed by others. If your company or your

FIGURE 1.2. Bull's-Eye

company's product is seen as that "thing you've just gotta have," it improves your brand, doesn't it? Think Apple. That's the essence of marketing in a very simplistic framework. Marketing is a process of selling product, promoting that product, placing the product in the appropriate classes of trade, and pricing it appropriately to generate profit for your shareholders.

In addition to improving an organization's brand awareness and brand recognition (yes, a company is in business to grow), key to a business is the ability to maximize its position against its competitors and to provide return on investment to its shareholders. We will get into this later in the book.

Having fun yet? I hope so because marketing is fun, pays well, and is a very rewarding career.

We could go in many different directions at this point, but let's keep it very foundational and we'll build from there. There are many different aspects of marketing that involve advertising, public relations, promotions, pricing products and services, placement (where do you want to sell your products/services?), and much more. However, for this chapter, we will focus on the four key marketing elements: product, placement, pricing, and promotion. Through the years, there have been additions to the elements of marketing (e.g., digital media, social media, etc.), but the basic elements are the same and have been since this wonderful area of business focus was introduced to the world.

I worked for Sony Electronics, Inc., and Samsung Electronics America for a period of time in my career. I was fortunate to work with some of the best marketing minds in the business, many wonderful, creative, and bright people. Marketing professionals everywhere will tell you that marketing is about communicating. Yes, it's that simple. (Really? Yes.) It's also about being redundant, repetitive in your communications and marketing message points. Why? I had the same question when I started my career at Sony. When the marketing groups (we had several) would get up in front of the company and speak about the upcoming year and what Sony's

FIGURE 1.3. Sony Building Tokyo

focus would be—for example, camcorders—I used to think, "How many times do you have to say that we're going to key in on these five features for 1998?" Our senior leaders would say and emphasize the same five key features in press releases. Do you know why marketing uses repetition? It's to drill the concepts and focal talking points into the sales team's head so that they do it when they are visiting with their accounts for line reviews. It's the same process, simple as it may seem, as when you tell a toddler "no" when he or she is too close to the edge of the staircase. At some point, even to a toddler, the repetition sends a signal that it's not safe to be by the staircase if you hear "no" repeatedly. The same logic applies to marketing messaging. You say it over and over to your audience. How many times have you seen a commercial saying the exact same thing about a product? You can think of several while reading this. How about print ads? How about billboards? You may be in several different cities, but the messaging is the same.

So, What are the Activities Associated with Marketing Goods and Services?

There are four generally accepted activities that are associated with marketing any product or service:

- Communicating information about goods and services.
- Making those products available to consumers.
- Pricing products and services appropriately to generate sales and profit for the company.
- Providing after-sales service to consumers.

COMMUNICATING INFORMATION

With marketing, you are communicating information about goods and services. Marketing messages must be:

- Clear
- Measurable
- Concise
- Repetitive

If your message to your audience isn't clear, then why do you do it? What's the purpose? You must have a goal in mind with your marketing message. What are you trying to accomplish? To whom are you trying to sell? What is the objective of the message?

I will never forget early in my career working for Sony. I was very fortunate to have been a part of introducing flat screen television to the US market. That's right. The meetings we had regarding what our key marketing messages seemed to never end. The meetings we had were to ensure that we were getting it right. What does that mean? Well, think about it. At the time, introducing flat-screen television was going to cost Sony a boatload of resources to do so. You see, Sony produced their own CRTs (cathode ray tubes). To introduce flat screen into the product mix meant a monstrous undertaking of changing tooling, the process of melting glass, how the aperture grill would be positioned in the tube, etc. It was going to be expensive. Therefore, the consuming public paying for a Sony FD (Flat Display) TV would be paying double the price of a normal, curved screen television. That's why it had to be introduced correctly.

The investment was unlike any Sony had ever seen previous to that point. So, we developed several key messages that we drilled into our sales team. These messages included how much better the overall picture quality would be with a flat screen TV, how much better the aperture grill and yoke of the TV would perform in a flat screen TV. The key was to show the consumer that our picture quality was, as we put it, the "reference standard." The point of this real-life example is that companies are making real investments. Our message was clear: our goal was simply to be the best television in the industry. Our purpose was simple: to continue to build brand loyalty and make money. And we did. I was a little part of a significant group of people who really made a difference. Quite honestly, there were many days where I felt unqualified or less than adequate, but that was also a good thing. Always be humble—it will serve you well in the long term. If you're genuine, people will know it. If you truly care, people will know it. Your competition in your company or otherwise can never outperform these qualities. They will always win out.

Next, if your marketing campaign isn't measurable, it's useless. If you can't measure success (or failure), you don't know where you are. You don't have any ability to calibrate your objectives and focus. You must be able to say that yes, this was an effective marketing campaign because we increased the company's market share on this series of products by +5% during the last fiscal quarter. If that isn't able to be done, you shouldn't spend the dollars because marketing must have a return on investment.

FIGURE 1.4. Libra Scale

To be effective, the message must be concise. Most marketing messages have a very clear end game in mind for the target audience. It may be a marketing campaign by Starbucks to have a flavor of coffee pushed so that sales of that particular drink are increased. Or it could be an in-and-out car service that pushes a synthetic oil versus a natural oil for your automobile. There are thousands of reasons for a company's objectives in marketing, but the most effective ones are very concise: selling one idea—not multiple ideas—in a campaign.

Have you ever seen a marketing message that is constantly repeated? Well, there's a reason for that. How many marketing messages can you think of off the top of your head, right now, that you know? Here are a few of mine (and I'll bet you know them too):

- "Ours does what theirs does for less than half the price"—Suave soap.
- "StarKist don't want tuna with good taste, StarKist wants tuna that tastes good"—StarKist.
- "Nothing runs like a Deere"—John Deere lawn tractors (one of my favorites).
- "Switch to Sprint and we will cut your bill in half"—Sprint (the attack ad against Verizon; did it work? We will get into this as a case study later in the book).

FIGURE 1.5. John Deere Tractor

There are many more, but you get the idea.

Repetition in marketing is done to ensure a message is consistently emblazoned in the consumer's mind. It's expensive to do this, but it is effective. The more times you and I hear something, the more we grow to believe it, accept it, and ultimately buy it.

MAKING PRODUCTS AVAILABLE TO CONSUMERS

This sounds so simple, doesn't it? Imagine, though, if the latest and greatest Apple Smartwatch was introduced into the market, but there was a problem with production. What would happen in that case? How would you feel about Apple, about your experience? It would be a big letdown, wouldn't it?

Companies that understand the supply chain and its importance within the marketing arena win. They understand inventory management is critical to ensuring a successful marketing campaign and that the consumer experience is maximized when product is available at the right time. One of the best companies as it relates to the supply chain is Walmart. They are masters of the process.

When companies have a great supply chain system set up, they are extremely focused on delivering product to consumers when consumers want it. It's a fine line to walk as a company because there are a myriad of forces working against you.

That is why we are talking about this marketing activity—it's important, but hard to manage.

Here's why inventory is difficult to manage as a company:

- If you are introducing a new product into the market, you have no history on the demand of that product; therefore, you are guessing the demand projections at introduction and weekly needs.

- Inventory carrying costs are very high. Warehousing products that are not "turning" (which means they are not selling at retail) are costing companies profit dollars by sitting in the warehouse and collecting dust.

- If a company is in the unenviable position of high inventory, in many cases, it will need to promote the product to move it through the warehouse and onto retailers' shelves. The promotion must be attractive enough to entice the buyer to take the risk of the inventory. In essence, this means that he or she feels the price paid for the product is sufficiently low enough that will allow their consumer to see the value and purchase the product.

PRICING PRODUCTS AND SERVICES APPROPRIATELY

Have you ever purchased a product, gotten it home, and were dissatisfied with the purchase? That is called buyer's remorse, usually caused when the item's price does not live up to the expectations of its utility. Every time you purchase an item, price is weighed against the value you perceive the item enhancing your life. It happens, literally, in seconds. People don't buy products, they buy needs.

By far, one of the most important—if not the most important—element consumers evaluate when they begin their process of purchasing a product or service is price. The price of an item is the main factor for most consumers as they contemplate a purchase; they must evaluate in their minds the price/value relationship for any given item. If that relationship is balanced, then the item will be purchased. If not, the item will not continue to be in their evaluation set of items.

Pricing also has ramifications to the organization. Pricing is very important within an organization's profit and loss statement. Developing your pricing strategy allows you, as the owner, to price your products that will allow for an appropriate margin and sales revenue goal. There are many factors at a level that go into the pricing of products that involve raw material costs, promotional costs, warehousing costs, and many more. How you price products has an immediate effect on the profitability of your company; the effect is to your top line revenue. Think of top line revenue as sales, that's it. It's the starting point for which all other expenses are calculated. In general, the higher your top line sales revenue is, the less of a negative effect all of the company's expenses will have. Being able to build your brand recognition and loyalty will go a long way in allowing you to price your products higher than your competition.

PROVIDING AFTER-SALE SERVICE TO CONSUMERS

Is after-sale service important to you? You bet it is. It is to everyone.

I once purchased a computer (brand to remain anonymous). I had a problem with it and had to take it back to the retailer where I purchased it. I had to sign up for a number to be seen. Then, I had to send off my computer for 10 days while it was repaired. What happened next? You guessed it: it came back and wasn't repaired properly. What did I do? Did I demand a refund for the product that I purchased? Yes. Did it take a long time for them to refund the purchase? Yes. Will I ever buy this brand again? No.

Think about that time you went to a restaurant and had horrible service. What was your impression of that restaurant after that experience? It's happened to all of us at one time or another. It doesn't feel good; it's frustrating and gives you a jaded perception of that restaurant.

A company can have wonderful products and horrible service. If this is the case, I can almost guarantee you that the company will not survive long term. There is too much competition willing to go the extra mile to ensure that their customers are taken care of. Think Singapore Airlines—consistent service at every level of the consumer's experience.

Service after the sale is absolutely imperative to a company's strategic planning.

FIGURE 1.6. Singapore Airlines Flight Attendants

So, Let's Look at the Individual Elements of Marketing and Get a Feel For What They Do and Why They Exist

PRODUCT

Product by far may be the most important element of marketing. If you don't have good products (and services), you don't have anything. Having the right products to offer to your target market is critical to any company's success.

I have a student who needed a job, and he asked me if he could cut my lawn. I was hesitant, quite honestly, but said yes. What was his product that he was selling me? Was it his lawn tractor? What was he selling? It was his service in this case. His product was his service. He did a fantastic job on my lawn, edged, weeded, etc. His product was excellent. He was marketing his product to me as a professionally manicured lawn, and his product proved to be very good. He listened to exactly what I wanted from him (I wanted the lawn cut very short because I am deathly afraid of snakes). All companies must do the same thing. Whether you're my student, Sony Electronics, Procter & Gamble, or Boeing, your product must be excellent or you won't be around long.

FIGURE 1.7. Young Man with Tractor

Successful companies find out what the needs of their consumers are, and then they build the product to provide to the end consumer. If you do this, you mitigate risk that your products will not be priced correctly, have the right feature content, and will sell through at retail. Unsuccessful products cost companies billions of dollars every year. Product is king.

PLACEMENT

Placement, in the marketing sense, simply means where you are going to sell your products. What is your distribution strategy? Distribution in this sense is synonymous with placement. Distribution also has a supply chain meaning, but in marketing, it means what classes of trade your product will be sold into. Placement is a very strategic part of the marketing plan because where you place your products is as important as how it's priced and promoted.

Let's look at a very quick example of placement in marketing and why it is so important: let's say that Sony Electronics just came out with a television product that actually is a hologram (a TV that is virtual, 3D, spatial). This would be unprecedented product, very expensive and high end, with high margin associated with it.

Where would Sony sell this product when it is first introduced into the market? Would they sell it to Joe's Electronics, Home Shopping Network, QVC? No, they would sell it to Best Buy, where there are experts in the field that can talk about the feature content of the products and where Sony would maintain higher margins. From this starting point, they (Sony) would slowly begin to expand distribution (or placement) to other classes of trade. Make sense?

PROMOTION

In marketing, promotion means one thing: spending money on products that need to be sold.

Promoting products is an activity that involves marking down the price of an item to ensure that it is more attractive to the consumer so he or she will buy it. Companies do not like to hold inventory on products; they like to move products through their supply chain. It's pretty clear why they want to do this as well. Holding on to products is expensive. You must warehouse the product, pay for inventory carrying costs, insure it, etc. So, it's always in the best interest of the company to sell through products quickly, as new introductions are always on the horizon.

FIGURE 1.8. Red "Sale" Sign with Red Bags

Promotions can come in many forms: in-store promotions, online promotions, discounts, price changes, and many more.

The key component of promotions in marketing is return on investment. On their profit and loss statements, all companies build in a line item called reserves. Reserves are built into a company in order to promote products that become stagnant or are just not accepted by the consumer. All products must move through the supply chain and sell to the end consumer (you and me).

PRICE

Certainly, one of the most controversial, debated, and hotly contested elements of the marketing elements is price. In organizations, the sales arm in most cases wants the best price for the product to ensure success in the marketplace. Marketing, on the other hand, is wanting profitability, and thus a higher price (and therefore higher margin).

So, how do marketers price products? How do they know how to price products in the marketplace? Well, herein lies a part of marketing that is arguably the hardest job in the marketing field—marketing research. Marketing professionals MUST know the competition, what like products are selling for, the history of like products, and the price erosion that happens within the product life cycle.

We will explore pricing and marketing research further in the book, but just know that price involves a lot of people, a lot of research, and a lot of discussion. It is extremely important, vital, to ensuring success with product introductions.

What is Utility, and Why is it Important in Marketing?

Quite literally, utility is the want-satisfying power of a good or service. Everything you use as a consumer during your 24 hours a day has utility or it doesn't. What you consume is either satisfying or it isn't.

FIGURE 1.9. Man Intently Shopping

Have you ever purchased a product and thought you got a fantastic deal on it, brought it home, unpackaged it, and started to use it? And it failed miserably? That is the definition of no utility. Or the item did not perform as advertised? In either case, your need was not satisfied. Your utility was zero.

Think about some of the things that you do by habit. Do you go to the same restaurant, same store, the same online e-tailer? Why do you do that? The same reason we all do: your needs are satisfied at those establishments where your needs are met over and over, and there is strong utility derived. Makes sense? Of course it does.

All companies, no matter the product or industry, all want loyal customers. Can you think of a more effective way to build brand loyal consumers for YOUR brand that are more important than providing consistent quality of product? The answer is no. Companies that are consistent with the quality of their product, developing innovation in their product line, and have strong service after the sale are the companies that succeed.

Can you think of any companies that have these traits? Apple, Starbucks, Nike, Coca Cola, Boeing … There are more, of course, but you get the idea. There are many companies where you know, as a consumer, you're going to have your needs satisfied every time you purchase or consume a product (or service) produced by these companies.

What is Marketing Myopia?

Marketing myopia happens in organizations. Marketing myopia is a situation in which a company becomes complacent in its efforts to maintain the edge or push the envelope in their marketing campaigns to gain market share.

There are many examples of marketing myopia. A great example of this is Sony Electronics. Sony was (and is) a fantastic consumer electronics icon. The company produced many products that we all know and love and continue to do so today. Products like the Walkman, Trinitron televisions, and many more catapulted Sony into the leading position within the electronics realm.

FIGURE 1.10. MiniDisc with Sony Logo

So, what happened? Sony became comfortable in their leadership position. Leaders should never become comfortable. There is always someone gunning for your market share position with new products, smart marketing campaigns, and focused distribution strategies.

Sony tried very hard to introduce products like the MiniDisc and others, putting a tremendous amount of marketing dollars on these products and neglecting others. They forgot their core business while they were diversifying their product line. During this time, there was also a consortium of companies that were intent on disrupting the way you and I listen to music and content. According to a September 24, 2012, article in the *Guardian*:

> By the time other labels began to see the benefits of MiniDiscs, it was too late. In October 2001, Apple launched its first iPod; meanwhile recordable CDs were becoming commonplace for those who wanted to make their own mixtapes. In 2001, both MiniDisc and cassette sales dropped by 70%, and the end for both formats was nigh. Die-hard fans continued to praise the device, but to no avail: in September 2011, Sony shipped the last MiniDisc Walkman—19 years after it had stumbled on to the marketplace. (Faulkner, 2012)

Apple and partners within their group were building a platform where you and I could download music over the Internet and not be hamstrung by physical products and media. Sony knew this was happening, tried to start formulating their own platform for music distribution over the Internet, and failed miserably. Again, as this was happening, efforts on core business with marketing and sales were not given the resources (marketing) to continue to compete and push brand loyalty. As a result, Sony suffered greatly with diminished market share across all of their core product categories: Television, Digital Imaging, Home, and Portable Audio.

Nonprofit Organizations and Marketing

In nonprofit, or not-for-profit organizations, the goal of marketing is to develop a loyal base of donors to the organization. The main impetus for marketing is to ensure that the company is funded through donations of other organizations and individual givers.

Marketing in this sense takes on an entirely different role, one of supporting a cause, a causal marketing initiative. How do companies do this?

FIGURE 1.11. St. Jude Children's Hospital, Memphis, Tennessee

Have you ever watched a St. Jude Children's Hospital television commercial (a great organization)? The goal of the television commercial is to inform you as to what St. Jude is doing to research childhood cancers/diseases, show the impact of what their research is doing to save lives, and, most importantly, to ensure the viewer knows that "no child will be turned away due to the inability to pay." That is powerful and endears the company to donors. The marketing campaign for St. Jude Children's Hospital and many others like it is to pull at your heartstrings to help children in need. Chrissy Paschall eloquently articulates the St. Jude mystique in her April 24, 2018, Virginia Tech Contributor article:

> Walking the expanse of the hospital my heart swelled in more ways than one. I saw moms with sunken smiles, kids with shiny heads, and doctors with heavy hearts. But not once did I see a single person with a loss of hope. St. Jude gives these families and these patients an unfaltering will to carry on. (Paschall, 2018)

What about PBS? Have you ever seen a PBS infomercial about its positive impact on television, how they focus on quality programming? How they are a league above the other programming? The goal for PBS is to be the broadcast station and member stations that provide trusted, informative, and educational programming. They do a great job of this and ask for our support to provide that programming. How does PBS market themselves if they are a nonprofit organization? They do it through donations from you and me. They also partner with well-known musicians, cooks, automobile companies, etc., who give of their time to help support PBS. During these "exclusive" programming spots, the PBS executives are on air, discussing the program and asking for support to provide you with excellent, trustworthy programming for years to come. It works.

In addition, the target market for nonprofit organizations is multifaceted. They target individual consumers as well as large organizations to help support their cause.

CHAPTER 1 REVIEW

By the end of Chapter 1, you should know the following:

- The definition of marketing.
- That marketing is a defined, repetitive series of messages aimed at your audience.
- The activities associated with marketing goods and services.
- The four main elements of marketing.
- The definition of utility.
- Marketing myopia: what is it, and why is it dangerous to organizations?
- Examples of nonprofit organizations.

Bibliography

Faulkner, Joey. 2012. "MiniDisc: The Forgotten Format." *Guardian*. https://www.theguardian.com/music/musicblog/2012/sep/24/sony-minidisc-20-years.

Paschall, Chrissy. 2018. "My Love for St. Jude." *Her Campus*, April 24. https://www.hercampus.com/school/virginia-tech/my-love-st-jude.

FIGURE CREDITS

KEY ELEMENTS IN THE MARKETING PROCESS

Business planning, or strategic planning, is the basis for all of the practices marketers employ while developing their business within the competitive realm where they engage. Strategic planning encompasses many elements that will determine if, where, and how a company will compete. There are many areas in which organizations must determine a "go" or "no-go" strategy. Once the decision is made based upon many aspects of the strategic plan, then it becomes very tactical to develop the correct focus and balance within the organization to achieve objectives that will sustain longer-term goals.

Developing the Strategic Plan

Any strategic plan depends upon knowing your audience and what you are intending to say to it. You must understand your target market (more about that in a minute). You need to know what you're trying to sell (we are all trying to sell something to someone every day). You should be able to communicate the clear marketing goals and objectives, first to your organization, then to the target market.

A company needs to ask several questions to fully understand whom to target and when:

- What are we trying to communicate?
- To whom are we trying to communicate?
- When will we communicate the marketing messages?
- What is the impact of our strategic plan on our target market?
- What did we accomplish? How will our strategic plan be measured?

The Strategic Window

The strategic window is the time frame when key requirements of a market and a company's core competencies best fit together. This is the strategic window—the time frame where the communication or introduction will be best received by the target audience you are trying to capture.

The strategic window of opportunity involves the timing of your marketing messages that correlate to a product introduction, a time of year, seasonality, or some combination of these factors. It can involve only one of these or all of them. It depends on the analysis of the internal and external environmental factors and core competencies at work to either help or hinder the message for maximum impact.

The importance of knowing your company's strengths, your weaknesses, the opportunities that exist, and the threats are key to being successful with regard to your strategic planning. One of the tools that all marketing professionals utilize while putting together their strategic plans is a SWOT analysis.

What is a SWOT Analysis, and Why Do I Need to Know About It?

A SWOT analysis is an imperative element to understanding your competition. A SWOT analysis provides managers with a critical view of the longer-term action necessary to compete, as well as the current threats to your company.

FIGURE 2.1. SWOT Analysis

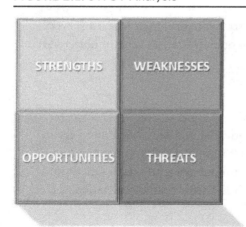

STRENGTHS

A company must understand fully their strengths. What are they good at, what do they excel at within the industry that they compete? Is it marketing in general? Are they the best at communicating a message? Are they great at supply chain/logistics? Do they have a great distribution strategy? A great sales force? What is it at the company that they know is superior to their competition? This is important to understand at all times.

WEAKNESSES

Conversely, and as important as strengths, a company must assess their weaknesses to understand the impact their strategic plan will have on their resources. If you don't have a great sales force, it would not be wise to introduce new products to your full distribution (classes of trade) at the same time. It would be more prudent to slowly introduce products as you have the manpower and capacity to train on the new products. Also, where do you need improvements that your competition would benefit from? This is a critical issue with many companies because, in many instances, your competition will know about your weaknesses at the same time you do. This is never a good thing; it can (and does, at times) open your company up to being extremely exposed to market share loss.

OPPORTUNITIES

Opportunities abound within business all around your company. There are always opportunities that can positively affect your business. They may be the demise of a competitor, a competitor having to raise prices, a relationship issue with a competitor's customers, etc. Opportunities can happen in multiplicity at varying times during the year, or there may be one opportunity that can help your company. In any event, it is always important to be cognizant of what is happening with your competitive landscape in order to capitalize on any missteps your competitors make. This may sound predatory or cold—and it is. You are trying to get a leg up on the competition any way you can (within reason, and most importantly, legally). You always want to ensure that you are on top of the current situation with your competitors and providing the best advice to senior management that allows your company to compete, gain market share, and add shareholder value.

THREATS

There are many threats that can develop as your company formulates its strategic plans. Threats can be internal, external, and may be situations that are unforeseen while putting your strategy in place. Threats can be the economy (domestic and global, if you're a multinational company); they can be monetary (devaluation of currency in companies you do business with); political (upheaval in countries where you compete); and internal (product quality, product availability, missing deadlines, relationship issues). The point is that threats are always there and need to be monitored, discussed, and contemplated as strategic plans are put together.

So, What Affects the Marketing Environment?

There are many variables that affect the marketing of products and services. Many of these variables are within a company's control, and many are not.

As we've briefly discussed, they consist of competitive, political, economic, technological, and sociocultural influences. All of these or just one can drastically affect your strategic planning initiatives and ultimately your marketing strategy.

The complexities of the environment within which a company competes will always dictate its strategy or strategies. The complexities multiply as you expand your business reach globally, and there isn't enough room in this book to discuss all of the pressures that can be exerted on companies. We will keep the discussion points to understanding how companies focus their efforts during a fiscal year.

FIGURE 2.2. Woman Presenting Sales Chart

In many instances, a company's focus may change from year to year. One year the organization may be focused on sales and the next they are focused on profitability. Both of these are important, but depending upon the resources available to the company, the focus will change.

Here's what I mean by that … If you have a great year introducing really fantastic products and you're knocking it out of the park (meaning that your sales revenue is great), as a company, for a couple years in a row, what you generally will be doing is making great strides in your market share gain. This is extremely important to a company for one reason (and an old Sony friend told me this)—if you're not growing, you're dying. That's true in a business sense. If your market share isn't growing, someone else is taking your market share, and that is never a good thing. Therefore, always improving sales revenue is important, as your improvement ensures that you are at least growing.

On the other hand, there are years where the focus is on profitability. When this happens, the company engages in practices that push technological advances or process enhancements in the organization that hopefully will improve the profitability. In most instances, a company will drive toward profitability when it is looking to improve its reserves cache, develop more products through research and development, or to enhance the company's stock price (Wall Street loves improved profitability!).

STRATEGIC BUSINESS UNITS

It's important for you to know that there are many facets or sub-organizations of a company that work in unison to achieve strategic planning objectives, and each of these has its own marketing plan as well. These sub-organizations, or divisions, are called strategic business units, or SBUs in business language. These SBUs are key business units within diversified companies. For example, Samsung Electronics America, Inc., is made up of many different SBUs. There is a division focused on television, one focused on digital audio, one focused on Samsung Telecommunications, and so on.

Each SBU has its own marketing plan; each must deliver top line revenue, and each must deliver bottom-line profitability to the organization. Each SBU has its own structure, resources, and management.

THE TARGET MARKET

Where do you want to sell your product or service? What is the makeup of the customer you want to sell to? What is their household income? What do they typically buy (what are their buying patterns)? How do they view your company/products?

All of the above are the elements of putting together your target market. The target market is the demographic where the company directs the majority of its marketing efforts. There will be nuances associated with target markets, but what marketing professionals do is isolate a general customer profile to whom they are focused on pushing their products. For example,

Walmart Stores, Inc.'s target market is "Mom"—that's right, "Mom." They gear their products' pricing and quality to provide Mom with exceptional value at the best possible price the market has to offer (which Walmart calls EDLP: Everyday Low Price). This is the way Sam Walton started the company and how current leaders at Walmart continue this mantra. Wikipedia describes everyday low price in the following manner:

> Everyday low price (also abbreviated as EDLP) is a pricing strategy promising consumers a low price without the need to wait for sale price events or comparison shopping. EDLP saves retail stores the effort and expense needed to mark down prices in the store during sale events, and is also believed to generate shopper loyalty. (Wikipedia, 2019)

This has been extremely effective ever since Sam Walton introduced America to Walmart in 1962. He based his company off of that premise then, and it holds to this day.

How do you define your target market, and does your target market, or target audience, ever change? The answer is that it depends upon what you're selling and who you think your customer should be. You must be extremely diligent about what you want your company to stand for and then decide on your targeted market. For example, Walmart for years had a slogan that everyone knew: "Always Low Prices." That was used for 19 years. After that

FIGURE 2.3. Walmart Sign

time, Walmart began using "Save Money. Live Better," which was later revised to "We Save People Money So They Can Live Better." The latter positioning has a folksy, I'm-talking-to-you-directly appeal.

So, What is the Difference Between Strategic Planning and Tactical Planning?

Strategic planning and tactical planning go hand-in-hand as companies develop their marketing plans. The only difference between the two is who, from the company's perspective, is responsible for the ownership and direction?

Strategic planning is setting the goals and objectives of the company. These are the higher-level, visionary focal points. They are usually set by the officers of the company, the senior-level executives. These are the "C Suite" folks who have the titles. These are the people who are setting direction, setting vision, and hoping that they have made the right decisions to set the company on a

FIGURE 2.4. Strategy versus Tactics

course to increased sales and profits. Strategic planning is usually drilled into the company employees from the top down. This sometimes feels almost dictatorial; however, in marketing, the key message points of a company must be repetitive and constantly reinforced by upper management.

The tactical planning function of the organization involves diving deep into the weeds of what needs to be done to actually see the strategy come to fruition. It's the nuts and bolts of the operation. These are the people who are doing the heavy lifting, the real work. They are mid-level managers focused on marketing research, consumer insights, shopper marketing, data mining, industry trends, etc. This is where the real work is done and where a lot of the unsung heroes of a company's success live. These are the real warriors of business. There is mad respect for these people, and they deserve every bit of the respect that they earn.

CHAPTER 2 REVIEW

By the end of Chapter 2, you should know the following:

- ■ What do companies need to understand when developing their strategic plans?
- ■ What is a strategic window of opportunity?
- ■ What are the definition and the elements of the SWOT analysis process?
- ■ What affects the marketing environment?
- ■ What are SBUs?
- ■ Explain a target market and how it is determined.
- ■ What is a strategic versus a tactical business plan?

Bibliography

"Everyday Low Price." 2018. Wikipedia, December 22. https://en.wikipedia.org/wiki/Everyday_low_price.

FIGURE CREDITS

CHAPTER 3

UNDERSTANDING THE COMPETITIVE ENVIRONMENT

As organizations develop their marketing plans, they absolutely must understand the competitive environment affecting their business. They need to know which marketing campaigns (how they work and why companies choose them) will be most effective. Should a company utilize print, broadcast, social media? What should they employ in order to be most effective in their efforts? In addition, as companies develop programs designed to enhance their brand position in the marketplace, you must also understand government regulations and agencies that are designed to keep consumers safe. Ethics in marketing is also a very large issue that should always be kept at the top of the list of an organization's priorities.

Identifying and Interpreting Trends in the Marketplace

Have you ever heard of a company called Circuit City? Have you ever wondered what happened to them? This was a multibillion-dollar organization, selling the latest and greatest technology on the planet. What happened? I ask again, what happened?

Here's what happened: Circuit City was competing head-to-head with Best Buy and ultimately could not compete. They filed for bankruptcy protection initially and then were done—not the Chapter 11 reorganization type. I'm talking about full-blown Chapter 7 liquidation.

Why, what happened? Circuit City lost its identity; they didn't define themselves to you and me, the end consumer. In addition, they made a myriad of mistakes that cost them market position, year over year, and ultimately the company. You could say that Circuit City developed an identity crisis while also suffering from marketing myopia. Chronologically, here's what occurred:

- They dumped sales of popular appliances. They got out of appliances, despite Circuit City having established itself as a destination.

- They spun off the CarMax portion of their business and, with it, a lot of talented management exited.

- Stores became too impersonal and too large.

- As Best Buy started to gain market share, Circuit City merely reacted and did not innovate on either its product or service side of the business.

- They stopped paying commissions to its sales force. (See a trend building here?)

- As a last step to avoid bankruptcy, they fired 3,400 of their most experienced salespeople ("Houston, we have a problem.")

- Wall Street discounted its share price.

- After Wall Street discounted the stock, Circuit City spent $1 billion in a stock buyback.

- Does the above project quality?

- No, it shows market myopia, poor decision-making, greed, and very poor quality.

- Circuit City filed for bankruptcy protection November 10, 2008, and ultimately went out of business, liquidating assets.

You need to understand this: trends represent significant opportunities or threats to the organization. They must be assessed continuously, ensuring that your company has the best information available to make prudent business decisions. Circuit City did not watch/understand the trends that were happening all around them.

FIGURE 3.1. Circuit City Storefront (Going Out of Business)

Understanding Marketing Decisions' Impact on the Company

Have you ever watched a commercial and tried to figure out why a company ran a particular commercial or ran an ad in the paper a certain way? Has that ever happened to you?

If you watch some commercials, the company sometimes comes directly at another company with an attack ad. We will review one of those commercials in a minute. As a side note, attack ads rarely do any good for the company that runs them. It is always viewed as just that, an attack on another company; a cheap shot.

Let's look at one of these ads, which happens to be one for Sprint.

Do you remember this guy?

FIGURE 3.2. Paul Marcarelli

His name is Paul Marcarelli. He was a broadcast pitchman for Verizon Wireless. If you remember the commercial that ran, what was the tag line? "Can you hear me now?" That's right, and do you remember the year the commercial first ran? It was 2002, quite a while ago.

Now, the most important question: was this commercial (and eventually a series of commercials) effective for Verizon? During the first year of "Can You Hear Me Now?" Verizon sales grew 10 percent. From the May 9, 2008, Blogspot Marketing Campaign Case Study:

> "Can You Hear Me Now?" was connected with some of Verizon's earliest and greatest successes, including reducing customer turnover to 1.8 percent, a 2.5 percent drop from 2000. "You can see that the commercials have really resonated with consumers," said Sue Marek, a former industry analyst who covered the wireless sector for Wireless Week, told the Baltimore Sun. "It's really paid off for them in a big way." While competitors had to drop prices to maintain market share, Verizon was able to maintain its average monthly service revenue per user at $49. During the first year of "Can You Hear Me Now?" Verizon sales grew 10 percent.

Verizon had two main goals for the "Can You Hear Me Now?" campaign: increasing the subscriber base and establishing itself as a premium service provider.

Consumers in 2002 were just as concerned about quality as they were about price. At that time, there was still a lot of coverage and dropped-call issues with cell phones, believe it or not. The "Can You Hear Me Now?" campaign was a huge success, increasing Verizon's market share, revenue, and profitability.

So, that's great, right? What about the attack ad that we're talking about? Well, here's what happened. Sprint, of all the carriers, has always lagged in market share to Verizon, AT&T, and T-Mobile. They are always number four in market share on average.

Sprint got the bright idea to attack Verizon with its "We will cut your bill in half" broadcast campaign. Guess who the Sprint pitchman is? You guessed it: Paul Marcarelli.

Sprint said that they will absolutely cut your bill in half and all you have to do is switch to Sprint. Well, according to a June 2016 *Wireless Week* article, the National Advertising Division (NAD) of the United States investigated the Sprint claims. Here's what they found:

They determined Sprint's claims were not possible because Sprint did not include activation and tax fees in quotes to customers and that "the overriding message—that you can have the same rate plan for half the price simply by switching to Sprint—was not supported by the evidence in the record and recommended that the commercials be discontinued." According to topclassactions.com, a February 15, 2017, article by Michael A. Kakuk points out that this, in fact, was the case:

> A class action lawsuit filed on Feb. 13 against Sprint Communications Inc. alleges that the wireless phone company misleads consumers with its "cut your bill in half" promotional advertising.

Further, and under the same article:

> Based on these misrepresentations, the class action asserts that Sprint committed multiple violations of the California False Advertising Act and the Unfair Business Practices Act.

Today, Sprint is still fourth among the large cell carriers due to slower data speeds, higher percentage of dropped calls, and spotty coverage.

What's the moral of the story? Attacks rarely work, AND customers are angry after realizing that the claims are false! And think of the marketing dollars that were spent on the broadcast campaign (by the way, you still see the commercials). These are bottom-line dollars that are not generating any market share increase to Sprint.

As a side note, as of this writing, T-Mobile and Sprint are in discussions to merge their companies. That would take the major carrier providers in the United States from four to three. Is this a good thing? Ask yourself that question. In most industries, reducing the amount of competition is never a good thing. In general, reducing the number of competitors in a market almost always translates to higher prices, worse service, and less innovation. We will see as we watch the merger discussions continue.

The Competitive Environment and Protection Laws

The business climate is extremely competitive, and consumers need to be protected. There is a myriad of laws that are put in place to protect you and me. There are government agencies that abound, focused on improving consumers' lives through safety and keeping companies honest.

Antitrust laws are designed to prevent restraints on trade such as business monopolies. We've seen many corporate leaders subpoenaed to discuss their business practices with Congress over the years. Some of these congressional hearings have been very well known. Bill Gates, for instance, appeared before the US Congress in 1998 to argue that his company, Microsoft, was not being monopolistic. His view was that no consumer would ever be required to pay a "transaction fee" for using Explorer. His contention was that every entrepreneur was free to compete within the very large ($100 billion at the time) software industry. According to a March 3, 1998, *Wired* article:

FIGURE 3.3. Bill Gates

"In the end, the software industry, which contributed over $100 billion to the national economy last year, is an open economic opportunity for any entrepreneur in America," Gates told the Senate Judiciary Committee. Government control, he said, would only restrict innovation."

There are many government bodies that are designed to protect us:

- The Drug Enforcement Agency protects us against illegal drugs entering into the United States for distribution.

- The Environmental Protection Agency protects us against environmental hazards and health hazards seen or unseen.

- The Consumer Product Safety Commission is designed to protect the public against unsafe products that have been introduced into the market (think Ford Pinto). Remember what happened with the Ford Pinto? The car was introduced into service by Ford as an inexpensive family sedan. However, there was a monumental flaw in the design. If the vehicle was hit from behind, the gas tank would explode because of the pressure and subsequent gas erupting onto the hot exhaust system. Ford, on July 9, 1978, recalled 1.5 million Ford Pintos and 30,000 Mercury Bobcats (same chassis) after 500 deaths and hundreds of injuries were linked to this flawed design. This debacle of an automobile design flaw was captured well by HowStuffWorks when they concluded:

In September 1978, Ford issued a recall for 1.5 million 1971–76 Pinto sedans and Runabouts, plus all similar 1975–76 Mercury Bobcats, for a safety repair. Each car received a new fuel-tank filler neck that extended deeper into the tank and was more resistant to breaking off in a rear-end collision. A plastic shield was installed between the differential and the tank, as well as another to deflect contact with the right-rear shock absorber.

In addition, the article went on to conclude that:

Ultimately, the trial judge had to dismiss the criminal charges. However, this was another stern warning not only to Ford, but to all of American industry regarding its responsibility for product safety.

- The Federal Aviation Administration oversees the maintenance and structural integrity of the airline industry.

- The Federal Trade Commission oversees business practices that are both domestic and international.

- The Federal Communications Commission monitors our airwaves and what comes in and out of them.

FIGURE 3.4. Ford Pinto

The newest regulatory frontier is cyberspace. There are a number of state and federal policing agencies, but the best known is the National Security Agency (NSA). Monitoring communications coming into the United States and transmitted out of the country are very high concerns for the safety of our citizens. This has become even more heightened and important over the years after 9/11 in 2001. Federal and state regulators are constantly investigating ways to police the Internet and online services.

In addition to homeland security, citizens' privacy and child protection issues are at the forefront of the difficult enforcement challenge—and make

FIGURE 3.5. National Security Agency Logo

no mistake, it is extremely difficult to police the Internet. The challenge is ever present and needs the full attention of thousands of professionals doing their best to keep America safe.

What About Ethics in Marketing?

Do marketers have an obligation to uphold the highest standard of ethics when planning and executing their marketing strategies? Of course they do, just like it's prudent to be ethical in everything we do as human beings. Within the business world, companies are always looking for the edge—the competitive edge. They are looking for a competitive advantage anywhere they can find it. In many instances, companies will walk a fine line of questionable ethics.

Well, how does that happen, and what exactly are we talking about?

Have you ever opened up a bag of chips (pick a brand, any brand)?

FIGURE 3.6. Photo of Doritos Chips

There is always a bit of a letdown when I do it: where are the chips? Why is the bag only half full of chips? I feel robbed, violated, taken advantage of; don't you? Not that big of an issue with you? It is to me, kind of a pet peeve of mine.

Companies will tell you that there needs to be a certain amount of "air" in the bag to lessen the crushing effect of shipping, or it's to keep the product fresh, etc. As a suspicious consumer, I think the reason there is a lot of space in the bags is to help the company's bottom line (spread the product out further and make more money). I could be wrong, but ...

What about marketing to children? This has come under increased scrutiny (think Brooke Shields and Calvin Klein) When Brooke Shields was 15 years old, Calvin Klein put several billboards and print advertising campaigns together showing Brooke, a child, in very provocative poses in order to promote their jeans. Who is the target market? Moms? Dads? Maybe 15-year-old males or females? Maybe both? The fact of the matter is that this advertisement is provocative, can be thought of (and was) as Calvin Klein taking advantage of Brooke Shields at a young age, exploiting her. In a twist of irony, Brooke Shields, now a 52-year-old mother of two daughters, has banned them from modeling until they are out of college. In a 1980 article, the Four A's industry publication cited the following regarding using Brooke Shields in the Calvin Klein jeans advertisement:

> Unfortunately, a scandalized America didn't consider Shields' appearance in the ads, looking much more mature than a mere 15-year-old "nothing". In fact, the ads caused a public uproar, making negative publicity as much a part of the marketing effort as the ads themselves. Though the commercial was banned by ABC and CBS in New York, Klein himself didn't back down from his choice.

Yes, there are many areas where there are questionable ethics—advertising to youth, product quality, planned obsolescence, brand similarity, packaging—they all can, and do, raise ethical issues with the public.

What About Truth in Advertising/Marketing?

Truth in advertising is the bedrock of ethics in marketing. Advertisers target certain products to different ethnicities, age groups, education levels, etc. The way advertisers target their messages to consumers has become increasingly sophisticated over the years.

Let's look at an example. How about reverse mortgages? To whom are they targeted? The affluent, younger couple doing well in their careers and in the middle-income tier of the United States? No. Then whom? Most reverse mortgage companies (wholly owned, insurance companies, etc.) target the older, lower-income section of the population. They are marketed as a solution to the seniors' financial cash flow problems; it's that simple. There have been several television spokespersons to tout the attributes of reverse mortgages, one of the latest being Tom Selleck. Remember him from *Magnum, PI*? Magnum PI was an action drama series starring Tom Selleck and was broadcast from December 11, 1980, to May 1, 1988. Mr. Selleck was seen, in the series, as a very trustworthy person and highly moral.

FIGURE 3.7. Tom Selleck

With a reverse mortgage, when you pass away or when the equity in the home has been used up, the reverse mortgage companies say the title of the home always stays with you; however; your equity in the home is gone as soon as the mortgage company makes the last equity payment to you. And the bottom line is that you are basically taking out a loan from the bank or insurance company. The fix is very short term, and you may have to sell the home to pay back the loan. Again, it's that simple. There are a number of alternatives for seniors to combat financial struggles. So, is this a truth-in-advertising issue for you? Is it ethical to push this on our senior community? You tell me.

What about companies that market to consumers with poor credit ratings? Do you think that happens? It happens every day. If you are a person with a poor credit rating, you are receiving direct-mail marketing that is in your mailbox on a regular basis from credit card companies offering you a credit card. First of all, how are these credit card companies able to know that you have poor credit? It's easy: many of these companies have access or buy access to credit rating reports. From there, they offer you a credit card, but with a catch. The credit card they offer you doesn't have an 11%–15% average percentage rate. Their percentage rates are in the high 20s and even 30+, and it gets worse if you default on the balance owed. These are called subprime interest rate carrying credit cards. What do you think about this? Is it legal to offer these credit cards at these rates? Absolutely, it is. Is it ethical to offer these credit cards at these rates? You tell me.

By the end of Chapter 3, you should know the following:

- Are trends important for businesses to understand?
- How often do companies assess industry trends where they compete?
- What type of commercial did Sprint run featuring Paul Marcarelli? Was it successful?
- Examples of federal laws protecting consumers.
- Understand questionable ethics in marketing.
- After reviewing the section on truth in advertising/marketing, know what to look for when viewing commercials that seem "too good to be true."

Bibliography

Auto Editors of Consumer Guide. n.d. "The Pinto Fire Controversy." howstuffworks. https://auto.howstuffworks.com/1971-1980-ford-pinto12.htm/.

"Brooke Shields Sparks Controversy in Calvin Klein Jeans." 1980. Four A's. https://www.aaaa.org/timeline-event/brooke-shields-sparks-controversy-calvin-klein-jeans/.

"Can You Hear Me Now? Campaign." 2008. Marketing Campaign Case Studies, May 5. http://marketing-case-studies.blogspot.com/2008/05/can-you-hear-me-now-campaign.html.

"Gates Urges Government to Leave Innovators Alone." 1998. *Wired*, March 3. https://www.wired.com/1998/03/gates-urges-government-to-leave-innovators-alone/.

Kakuk, Michael A. "Sprint Class Action Challenges 'Cut Your Bill In Half' Promotion." Top Class Actions. February 15, 2017. Accessed May 24, 2019. https://topclassactions.com/lawsuit-settlements/lawsuit-news/489077-sprint-class-action-challenges-cut-bill-half-promotion/.

FIGURE CREDITS

E-COMMERCE AND THE DIGITAL WORLD

E-commerce is a very broad term that just means transactions that take place on the Internet. It is these transactions that have allowed small Mom-and-Pop companies to become truly global, by virtue of selling and transacting over the Internet: e-commerce. The growth of online sales over the last decade is phenomenal. According to the February 2019 (updated March 2019) issue of *Digital Commerce 360*, consumers spent $453.46 billion on the web for retail purchases in 2017, a 16.0% increase compared with $390.99 billion in 2016. That's the highest growth rate since 2011, when online sales grew 17.5% over 2010. E-commerce is here to stay, and companies that continue to hone their skills at marketing digitally will be poised for growth. Specifically, the issue cited the following growth rate for e-commerce for the time period:

> E-commerce retail sales increased by 16% to $453.5 billion in 2017, accounting for 8.9% of total retail sales for the year, according to a U.S. Census Bureau report released on February 16, 2018. ... The growth was due in large part to brick-and-mortar retailers' active investment in omnichannel platforms. E-commerce retail sales include both the revenue of pure-play "e-tailers" and the online sales of primarily brick-and-mortar brands. It is growth in online sales of the latter group that is driving overall growth in e-commerce sales, as providing omnichannel remains the key to success for all retail brands.

There will always be physical storefronts, but marketing digitally to you and me will continue for the foreseeable future.

Okay, So What is E-commerce?

E-commerce simply describes a wide range of business activities that take place via Internet applications. The Internet has been a monumental success. However, issues and concerns relating to e-commerce remain, both from a business standpoint and for consumers who purchase products over the Internet.

FIGURE 4.1. Monitors with Digital Background

The largest issue for retailers is the unauthorized selling of their brand on .com and the counterfeiting of a brand's products on the web. Retailers who sell over the Internet are (and should be) very protective of their brand. When unauthorized resellers are selling their products over the Internet, the brand can be devalued, as unauthorized resellers are not concerned about the brand's worth in the marketplace. They will sell the brand for whatever price they can get for it, even if it is very disruptive.

In much the same way, consumers have issues about the Internet as well. The largest issue for consumers is that they are very leery of providing private information about themselves over the Internet. Think about it: even today, do you get somewhat nervous about providing your Social Security number, your driver's license number, your credit card information, over the Internet? I sometimes do, but less and less as web security systems increase.

FIGURE 4.2. Online Shopping

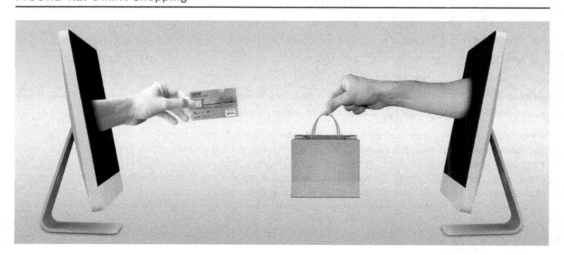

The bottom line is that the benefits and potential of e-commerce far outweigh the concerns and problems for both retailers and consumers. In addition, over time, the percentage increase of people who shopped online versus going into a physical

FIGURE 4.3. Amazon Logo

store is growing dramatically. During the fourth quarter of the year, online shopping drastically increases as consumers shop for back-to-school items, Halloween, Black Friday, Cyber Monday, and Christmas. What e-tailer was the big winner over the holiday selling season in 2018? Amazon, by far ... no one else even came close.

What Activities Take Place Over the Internet?

There are many activities that take place over the Internet; however, e-commerce can be divided into five broad categories:

- Business-to-consumer transactions
- Business-to-business transactions
- Electronic data interchanges (EDI), or digital data flow
- E-mail, instant messaging, blogs, podcasts, and other web-enabled communication tools
- Education and researching products for potential purchase

Business-to-consumer transactions are exactly what the phrase implies. These transactions are specifically transacted between an e-tailer (e.g., Amazon, Wayfair, Walmart, etc.) and you and me, the end consumers. An example of this is when you visit Amazon Prime and purchase a product or buy any other item directly from any other business website. This is considered a business-to-consumer transaction, and these types of transactions happen millions of times a day.

Business-to-business transactions are e-commerce transactions that take place between a business and another business. This type of transaction is a bit more complex than a consumer transaction because there are different types of reasons businesses sell to other businesses. There are times when businesses purchase products from other businesses that are directly related to selling products. An example would be Ford Motor Company purchasing Yokohama tires for their cars. The purchase is between businesses, but the true end consumer, you and I, has not been involved at this point. Another example of a business-to-business e-commerce transaction would be Boeing, Inc., purchasing paint from DuPont Chemicals to paint its airplanes. Again, the end consumer is not involved at this point.

How about EDI, and what does that mean? EDI (electronic data interchange) is a data flow system that most larger companies use to "talk" to each other in terms of sales, inventory, product flow, etc. This is very widely used among businesses and retailers to ensure that both the flow of product and production is clear, but also the data involved in the supply chain process of moving goods from the manufacturer to the retailer.

E-mail, instant messaging, blogs, podcasts, and other web-enabled communication tools are vital to support all businesses in one way: communicating important information necessary to fulfill consumer's needs. This area of Internet activity is vast and has a lot of moving parts, but suffice it to say that this area of e-commerce activity is solely devoted to effective, timely communication.

Education and researching products for potential purchase is one of the most sought-after reasons consumers use the Internet. Did you know that over 75% of consumers research products online before they purchase them? That's amazing, isn't it? I know I research. There are many tools that are available for consumers to be able to educate themselves on a do-it-yourself project, or sift through product reviews, or compare pricing, etc. There are literally hundreds of sites devoted to helping you educate yourself on virtually every topic that you can imagine.

What About Proprietary Information, and is it Important?

Proprietary information means that it is owned. Many aspects of a business can be "owned" and are owned. Proprietary doesn't just involve products and information. It can be as simple as the formula for a product, an icon, image, name, schematic for an audio device, etc.

Have you ever seen a registered trademark or trademark symbol listed after a brand or sub-brand? That means that it has been registered with the federal government, and that it is owned. It cannot be duplicated in any way, shape, or form. Think of Apple: do you think they protect their proprietary icon (the apple symbol with a bite out of it)? Of course, they do. They fiercely protect this symbol, as well as many patents that they hold. According to an April 21, 2017, article by Mohd Azad in *Quora* magazine:

> Apple already makes more from its logo every month than most other companies in the world. A good majority of its customers buy Apple products only because of its logo.

Apple, yes, is keenly aware of the power of its logo.

What about Coca-Cola? Do you believe that the formula for Coke is written down somewhere in a very secure vault? Yes, it is. Aleksandar Mishkov discovered the vault and reported on it:

> Coca Cola's recipe is one of the best kept business secrets of the past decade. Competitors have tried to imitate and mimic the taste and flavor of Coca Cola, but they've failed over and over. The company tries hard to keep the secret hidden. There is a myth that only 2 people have ever seen the secret formula. But no matter how many people have seen the formula, one thing is certain, the company has gone above and beyond to protect the recipe from prying eyes. In fact, the company has its own high-tech vault that holds the recipe.

These are somewhat simple examples; however, a company's proprietary information is no laughing matter; it's serious business. AND companies protect their proprietary information vehemently. It is a matter of life and death to a company. Remember, as we have said, every company within the industry or industries that you compete with are ALWAYS after your market share. Always!

- Pricing
- Policies/processes
- Customer lists
- New product introductions yet to be released
- Intellectual property (what is this?)
- Patents
- Patents pending
- Patent applications

And the list goes on and on. Proprietary information is very important to organizations, and there is a singular goal: to protect the company brand and sensitive information.

What Types of Challenges are There Regarding E-Commerce?

There are significant channel conflicts and copyright issues that can develop within e-commerce. As we will learn, channel conflicts mean the retail or e-tail conflicts. These conflicts can be wide and varied, as we will see.

Of the many challenges that arise, the main issues that organizations face with regard to e-commerce are pricing, promotions, product mix, and channels of trade/distribution. These are a few of the areas that are constantly an issue with marketers transacting business online.

SO, WHAT KINDS OF ISSUES HAPPEN WITHIN EACH OF THESE AREAS?

Pricing is by far the largest single issue that can have a damaging effect on an organization. Manufacturers set a suggested price for the market on every one of the models that they produce. This is called a manufacturer's suggested retail price, or MSRP. Based upon their knowledge of the market, this is where the organization feels the product should be priced at retail and where a retailer can reasonably set the competitive price and make a profit. The one thing that you should always bear in mind, however, is that a retailer is free to set the price of their products for whatever price they deem is appropriate. No manufacturer can dictate that to a retailer. It's against the law. We could go on and on about pricing, and there are many meetings that do just that. The key point to note in this area of challenges is that pricing is very sensitive to every manufacturer because major fluctuations in price in the market can have very damaging consequences to their bottom line (their profitability).

Promotions can be both positive and negative to an organization. Promotions are any vehicles designed to help sell a model or a series of products in the market. For example, assume you are Vizio, Inc., and you have a 50-inch smart TV that has been lagging behind the competition in sell-through. What do you do? First, you need to understand the market (understand the competition is another way to say this). You need to know why your 50-inch smart TV is not selling well versus the competition. It could be that the feature content is less than the competition, or it could be an older model when competition has new product on the shelves. There are a myriad of reasons that could place this product in an over-inventoried situation. So, what do you do? You need to promote the item (i.e., you need to mark it down—lower the price of the product so it is more attractive to the consumer). So, does this affect your bottom line? You bet it does because you're burning dollars to help sell through the product. But does it also help you? Yes, because it helps your relationship with your retailer, and it also helps deplete inventory to make way for new products. The most important of these is the relationship with your account base. Without a great relationship and trust, you have nothing.

How a company distributes its product mix to the classes of trade they sell to can be a challenge. A company's product mix is their portfolio of products that they have to offer its customers. Many times, if a manufacturer is selling its products, they want to keep brick and mortar (stores) versus e-commerce separate and independent of one another. That is very hard to do because retailers want to have all of the product mix a company offers on their website. It gives credibility to their company to have all products; it allows them to compete with Amazon (they always have all products available), and it adds to their cache of product offerings (very important for an online site to offer a wide range of products).

SO WHY IS THIS A CHALLENGE? DOESN'T EVERYBODY WIN IN THIS SITUATION?

No; in most instances, the manufacturer is always the loser. The manufacturer is always very careful of the "exposure" to their brand. And if there's anything we know, the Internet offers huge exposure, good or bad. Okay, so why is this an issue? Imagine you're a very strong brand, you sell a lot of product into a certain retailer, and they see their products mirrored at another retailer that also sells online. This is an issue because the retailer you sell a lot of product to (let's just call them your largest account) is not going to like their same product mix proliferated into the marketplace. They are going to object, trust me. Therefore, the key position to take is one of necessity to grow. All corporations need to grow—every one—no exception. This is a fundamental, systemic challenge to the way companies expand their product mix. It is always a challenge and always will be as long as companies continue to grow and expand their distribution.

Finally, another challenge with respect to e-commerce involves distribution channel strategy. Remember, distribution channel strategy in a marketing sense means where a company distributes its products. It's not the movement of goods; it's class of trade that is important here.

All manufacturers must decide where they are going to distribute or sell their products. It is their right to grant or refuse to sell a customer. There are many reasons that corporations evaluate whether they will sell their products or a subset of products to a retailer or online retailer. Some of those decisions involve what kind of exposure a retailer or online retailer poses to an organization's brand.

WHAT DOES THAT MEAN?

In the most simplistic terms, manufacturers or organizations do not want online partners that are not respecting their brand. What this means is they do not want the exposure of having their brand sold for less than what they feel the true MSRP is for the product. MSRP means

Manufacturer's Suggested Retail Price. Now, it must be stated that any retailer has the right to sell their products at whatever price they deem necessary to be competitive. That's the law, and it's there to protect retailers. What inevitably happens is a manufacturer will sell a retailer a product at $50 and the MSRP for the product as suggested by the manufacturer at $100, for example. However, if the retailer or online retailer wants to sell the product at a much lower price than $100, then MSRP goes right out the window.

So, how do retailers ensure that the integrity of their products and pricing stay intact? In a nutshell, it's an extremely difficult and delicate subject to broach with any retailer by a manufacturer. However, manufacturers do have a tool, and that tool is called MAP (minimum advertised price).

OKAY, SO WHAT IS MAP?

MAP, or minimum advertised price, is just that: it's the agreed-upon price a reseller agrees to advertise a brand or product for at retail. When a retailer accepts the MAP agreement, they're bound by the letter of the law in the contract. They can't advertise a product for sale any less than the agreed price. This means in print, online, or anywhere. Of course, this doesn't mean they can't sell the product cheaper; they simply can't display a cheaper price. In addition, pricing the product(s) at a lower price based upon a MAP policy or agreement will mean that any time a lower price is in the store means that it isn't shown or advertised, so it's hard to discover it.

CHAPTER 4 REVIEW

By the end of Chapter 4, you should know the following:

- The definition of e-commerce.
- Examples of drawbacks to e-commerce.
- Activities that are most common taking place over the Internet.
- Business-to-consumer transactions.
- Business-to-business transactions.
- What does EDI mean?
- Do consumers research products over the Internet before purchasing in-store?
- What does proprietary mean?
- List examples of proprietary information.
- What are some challenges within the e-commerce market?

Bibliography

Ali, Fareeha. 2019. "US E-commerce Sales Grow 15.0% in 2018."Internet Retailer, March 13. https://www.digi-talcommerce360.com/article/us-ecommerce-sales/.

Mishkov, Aleksandar. n.d. "Coca Cola Vault: Where Is the Secret Formula Kept?" documentarytube.com. http://www.documentarytube.com/articles/coca-cola-vault-where-is-the-secret-formula-kept.

FIGURE CREDITS
Fig. 4.1: Source: https://pixabay.com/en/monitor-binary-binary-system-1307227/.
Fig. 4.2: Source: https://pixabay.com/en/ecommerce-selling-online-2140603/.
Fig. 4.3: Source: https://commons.wikimedia.org/wiki/File:Amazon.com_Logo.png.

B2B, B2C, AND CONSUMER BEHAVIOR

There is a difference between marketing to a business and marketing to a consumer. Many of these are fundamental differences, and some are less discernable. When marketers design strategies around business-to-business, they structure their strategies to a more informative approach rather than selling. The focus is to provide other businesses with knowledge about your expertise in an industry. With business-to-consumer strategies, the focal point is individualistic, creative, and pushes toward the emotional aspect of marketing products. In a sense, it's classic marketing. Within these two differing viewpoints, consumer behavior plays a part in how you develop your strategic plans.

So, Let's Get Started—What The Heck is Business-To-Business Sales?

B2B means business-to-business. That's all. Not scary at all, and it just means that the sales transactions are from one business to another. The way in which a business "sells" to another business is very different from the way a business "sells" to the end consumer, you and me. So, what's the major difference?

When businesses market to other businesses, their main goal isn't to sell an actual product so much as to sell their leadership, their expertise in a certain field or industry within which they compete. Products that are sold within the B2B arena are generally more complex, take longer to sell in, and involve more people in the organization in the decision-making process.

Think of it this way: if I'm the Boeing Company, my customers are Delta and American Airlines. When I am bringing a new airplane to market, or a new engine, or new advancement for flight stability, the process of selling to these businesses (airlines) is very complex. Structural engineers, aeronautical engineers, marketing, designers, finance professionals, chief pilots, etc., are all involved in the selling process. It's extremely complicated; many relationships are entwined, and it takes a much longer time to close the sale.

This is the essence of B2B selling. There are a myriad of people/professionals involved in the process, and the product is much more complex than B2C (which we will discuss next).

Okay, so you get that companies like Boeing, Caterpillar, and Alcoa Steel are involved in a complex selling experience. So how does it work with business-to-consumer?

Business-To-Consumer Sales

The marketing of products in the business-to-consumer realm, or B2C, is very clean, fast, simple, and more emotional than B2B. So, what's the difference? What does the transaction look like?

To begin with, B2C transactions take place very quickly. Did you know that on average, consumers who find the type of product they are looking for on the shelf at any given retailer make their decision which one to buy within three seconds? Three seconds! That's amazing and true. Products within the B2C arena are wide and varied. We're talking toilet paper, facial tissue, toothpaste, laundry detergent, etc. These are products that are in many cases necessities, not nice-to-haves. Consumers also are not dealing with complex business relationships along the path to purchase. Transactions are fast, don't require a lot of thought, and satisfy short-term needs versus the longer-term needs in the B2B environment.

While the B2C initialism identifies transactions between businesses and consumers at both physical store and online locations, B2C has been used primarily to describe the relationship that occurs online, same as B2B.

In B2C selling, the company is trying to engage with the end consumer in a way that strikes an emotional chord toward their brand. That is why it's so important for the businesses website to be as robust and engaging to the consumer as possible.

This need has sparked an entire industry of shopper marketing companies that says things like "ethnography," "thought leadership," "First Moment of Truth," etc. The need for these organizations has waned, except for within the digital space as our "path to purchase" continues to lead us more away from the storefronts and more toward online buying. In fact, in a December 2017 Marketing Industry Spending Study performed by the Cadent Consulting Group, they cite that "Shopper/Account-Specific Marketing [is] generally declining in retailer effectiveness with the exception of Sampling/Demos." Here, directly from the 2017 Marketing Industry Spending Study Executive Summary:

Shopper Marketing, which had recently been growing, appears to have plateaued. Having more than doubled between 2012 and 2014 (6.0% up to 13.5%), Shopper and/or Account Specific Marketing is resting at about 13% of total spending. Importantly, effectiveness ratings among retailers have fallen sharply, -27 points in 2016 to 65%.

The bottom line: no one cares what your ethnography study shows if you can't provide great product at a great price/value relationship to the end consumer, as well as articulate clear, measurable results that help a business grow. Period. Everything begins and ends with products and relationships. Everything. All else is just selling air, which doesn't benefit anyone.

I've always wondered why large corporations that have great marketing minds need to venture outside their companies for help with shopper marketing when the brainpower is right inside their organizations. B2C is a fantastic way for consumers to educate themselves, research products, and compare pricing. We all do it—it's fun, and it helps save us money, learn about products, and provides the education we need for a particular situation.

How About Consumer Behavior—What is This, and Why Does it Matter?

Consumer behavior is the study of individuals, groups, or organizations and the processes they use to satisfy needs. Consumer behavior drives the actions of consumers. Consumer behavior is how you and I got to be who we are; it's that simple. It's not a hard concept. It's your life, what you like to do, who you hang out with, who influences you, what makes you tick.

I will never purchase anything other than a Ford truck when I'm in the market for trucks. Why? There are a lot of great trucks that are out there. What would influence me to the point where I am so brand loyal to Ford? You know the answer. My dad only drove Ford trucks, and I would feel horrible if I purchased anything other than a Ford. He was my influencer, my idol, and my Dad. I would never go against him in anything. I also drive a Mercedes, but I'm good there, right? Please tell me that's okay.

I have also been very concerned about finances, "making it," and being "okay in retirement." Why have I been like this? I grew up in a family of 10 people—yes, 10 people. Five brothers and three sisters. My father worked hard for our family, and we were well taken care of but never had any money. No one had to tell me I was going to go to college. I knew I was going, and I knew I was going to be paying for it. Why was that so important to me? Because I was scared to death about not having enough money because I saw it as I grew up. I became an overachiever, whatever that truly means these days.

Okay, let's get back on track before I start to tear up.

So, what affects consumer behavior for you and me? What is it that makes us buy what we buy? Short answer: it's complicated. Long answer: you have values, beliefs, preferences, attitudes, and tastes that all affect what you buy, how you buy, and where you buy. Some of you reading this section are nodding your heads saying "yes, I do buy a certain brand or type of car because of how I was raised, or this or that person was influencing my decision." We all do have influencers who affect our buying habits.

So, what about children as they relate to consumer behavior? Do children influence buying decisions? They absolutely do.

The family structure has changed over the last century. Here's how:

- Growing numbers of couples are separated or divorced.
- Single heads of household are more common.

The role of each spouse (or significant other) in a household has also changed:

- Autonomic role (unconscious decisions).
- Husband-dominant role.
- Wife-dominant role.
- Syncretic role (joint decisions).

TABLE 5.1. Percent Distribution of U.S. Households by Type, 1940–2010

Household Type	1940	1960	1980	2000	2010
Family Households	90.0	85.1	73.7	68.1	66.4
Married couples with children	42.9	44.3	30.7	23.5	20.2
Married couples without children	33.4	30.5	30.2	28.1	28.2
Single parents with children	4.3	4.1	7.2	9.2	9.6
Other family	9.4	6.2	5.6	7.1	8.5
Nonfamily Households	10.0	15.1	26.4	31.9	33.6
One person	7.8	13.4	22.6	25.8	26.7
Other nonfamily	2.2	1.7	3.8	6.1	6.8

Note: *Percentages for subcategories may not sum to category totals due to rounding.*
Source: *U.S. Census Bureau, decennial censuses from 1940 to 2010.*

PERCENT DISTRIBUTION OF US HOUSEHOLDS BY TYPE, 1940–2010

If you look at the above chart, the key statistics to note are that married couples with children are down 52% and single parents are up 223% since the census has been going on. What does that tell you?

There are a lot of children dependent on and influencing single parents.

- **Single-parent households are growing.**
- Some are the result of divorce.
- Some are by choice.
- **Single parents want to please children.**
- And therefore initiate their engagement.
- And value their input.
- Single parents view children as their "friends."

Regardless of the circumstances, single parents are more likely to engage their children in purchasing decisions.

Let's Talk About Influencers

Influencers are the trendsetters. These are the people who purchase new products before others in a group and then influence others in their purchases. I'm not talking about early adopters in this section. Many people confuse influencers and early adopters. Early adopters are the people who want the latest and greatest technology. They want the newest gadgets, etc. Influencers act as opinion leaders based on their knowledge of and interest in products but from a different point of view: yours, not theirs.

FIGURE 5.1. Matthew McConaughey

The definition (https://study.com/academy/lesson/opinion-leader-in-marketing-definition-lesson-quiz.html) of an opinion leader "is a well-known individual or organization that has the ability to influence public opinion on the subject matter for which the opinion leader is known. Opinion leaders can be politicians, business leaders, community leaders, journalists, educators, celebrities, and sports stars." You can also have family opinion leaders—again, my father was my opinion leader.

Who is this guy? What's his name, and what is he selling? Does his opinion matter? Yes, of course it does. It's Matthew McConaughey, and he's selling Lincoln Continentals. Who's he selling the car to? Is it the 65–75-year-old male? No, Lincoln already has that buyer locked down, and they're pretty brand loyal as well. Okay, so who is he selling this vehicle to? He's selling it to a younger crowd, the 45–55 year-old male. Matthew McConaughey was 44 years old when the commercials began. Is that it then, younger 40-something males? No, they're also selling the car to the female population that also influences their husbands. So, have the spots been successful?

According to the blog *Hollywood Branded* in an October 18, 2017, article, sales of Lincoln Continental were up 13% since the inception of the commercials featuring Matthew McConaughey started in 2014. The article cited McConaughey's strong influence in the success of Lincoln Continental sales:

> Lincoln reports that their sales were up by 13 percent year-to-date at the time of [its] release. Arguably, this is a huge turn around for Lincoln considering the commercials had only been in circulation for approximately two months before they saw sales jumps. McConaughey's partnership with Lincoln was directly attributed to the success and bump in sales. Lincoln reported that the newly released vehicles were warmly received by auto-critics. Since the MKC first hit dealerships in May 2014, U.S. sales have steadily increased.

What About Reference Groups?

Reference groups are people whose opinions you value above all others. These are groups of people you look to for guidance, approval, and acknowledgment regarding your behavior, how you look, what's important to you, and your conduct. Reference groups are a standard or frame of reference, how you order your experiences, perceptions, and ideas of "self."

Okay, so we'll just go there. Some of you reading this book belong to a sorority or a fraternity. Do you see your fellow members as a reference group for you? You probably do. Imagine walking into your sorority or fraternity house and noticing that they all wear a certain color or brand of pants, shoes, or shirt. Would this influence you to possibly purchase it? I would say that it would.

Reference groups can also be your family. Why are you going to college? Is it because your entire family has gone to college? Is it because one person in your reference group has been more positively vocal for you to attend and you value this person's opinion more? You see him or her as the standard; therefore, attending and graduating with a college degree is more palatable?

Reference groups can also be very formal in nature. They can have a specific goal or mission. They also have a specific structure and positions of authority. There are many examples of formal reference groups, such as MADD (Mothers Against Drunk Driving), the NRA (National Rifle Association), HOG (Harley Owners Group), AMA (American Marketing Association). These are groups that are designed to have specific goals in mind; they have an organized structure, and they serve as a reference group for many people who have the same ideas or beliefs about a topic or topics that are important to you.

CHAPTER 5 REVIEW

By the end of Chapter 5, you should know the following:

- **What are the main differences between marketing to businesses versus marketing to consumers?**
- **What is the definition of consumer behavior?**
- **Know what the changing household structure is in the United States. What are the trends?**
- **How are children influencing the households where there is a single parent?**
- **What are influencers, what do they do, and what is another name for an influencer?**
- **What is a reference group?**

Bibliography

"2017 Marketing Spending Industry Study." http://cadentcg.com/wp-content/uploads/2017-Marketing-Spending-Study.pdf.

Tawater-Tiedemann, Alexis. 2019. "How Matthew McConaughey Increased Sales for Lincoln." *Hollywood Branded* (blog), March 4. https://blog.hollywoodbranded.com/blog/how-matthew-mcconaughey-increased-sales-for-lincoln.

FIGURE CREDITS

TARGET MARKETS AND SEGMENTATION

Okay, so let's explain what target markets are and why it's important for marketers to clearly identify their target market. In a very succinct sense, target markets are groups of people a company believes would be the most attractive and, more importantly, most active purchasers of its products and/or services. Target markets can be large, small, global, local, multiethnic, ethnic-specific, etc. You get the picture: target markets can be very different, depending on what consumer need the organization is trying to fulfill. You belong to a target market for many different companies. You are in the "sweet spot" due to your preferences, your habits, your fondness for a brand, or your brand loyalty. There are many different reasons for being a part of a target market, but the key is that companies know how you buy, where you buy, what you buy, and when you buy. Kinda scary, huh?

Types of Target Markets

There are two main types of target markets that marketing professionals focus on. Consumer markets focus on end consumers of their products for personal use. These are items such as toothpaste, shoes, hamburgers, soft drinks, etc.

Business markets focus on goods and services that are purchased directly or indirectly in the production of products for the end consumer. These are goods and services purchased directly or indirectly in the production of other goods and services for resale.

Think of the business markets as the following:

- Plastics for toothpaste tubes.

- Rubber for soles of shoes.

- Bulk meat for hamburgers (Tyson).

- Carbonation for bottlers that add syrup.

Think of products within the business market as items that aren't THE final goods, but a PART of the final good (product). They are critical for the product's success, but they are only a part of the product.

FIGURE 6.2. Tyson Foods, Inc. Headquarters

The end game for both consumer and business target markets is the same: understanding the competitive environment, understanding who your company serves, and understanding the wants and needs of the target market you have selected.

Given the volatility of the economy, having a well-defined target market is more important than ever, although we all know that ensuring you're right on your target market is mission critical. No company can afford to target everyone. Most companies do not have the resources to target every consumer. However, smaller businesses can effectively compete with large organizations by targeting a niche market.

Let's Look at Examples of Target Markets

Can you think of any company's target market? What about Target Stores? It's the "mini-van driving suburban mom," and they call her their "guest." They have also identified the Hispanic mom as their defined target market. From a March 4, 2015, article in the Business Section of the *Washington Post*:

> It was the era when it became common for loyal customers to affectionately refer to it as "Tar-zhay," a tongue-in-cheek French pronunciation that captured how they felt about the brand: It delivered a luxe shopping experience, even though the prices were low. In a presentation to investors this week, Target executives said its core customer at that time was the "Boomer Mom," someone who "drives a minivan," "lives in the suburbs" and "wants it all."

What about Walmart Stores, Inc.? Who is their target market? It's Mom. As confirmed by a January 27, 2011, article in *Forbes* magazine:

> Moms control over 80% of household spending, making them the "essential" consumer in America and Wal-Mart's target audience. "Wal-Mart is the biggest marketer to moms on the planet," says Wintsch, noting that her agency produces over 100 television commercials a year for the retailer.

Walmart is known for two things: low prices (or Everyday Low Price, to be exact) and very broad product assortments. They are excellent at giving their target market, "mom," choices and value. And, yes, they are true to their tag line of saving you money, so you can live better.

FIGURE 6.3. TruGreen Lawn Service

These are very large corporations, but how about a very small company? Do they really need a target market? You bet they do. All companies need to identify who they are selling to and why. What about a lawn service? Have you ever driven around and seen the many different logos of lawn service or landscape companies on the sides of trucks?

Sure you have. So, are their target markets different? Sure they are. One could only like to service the lawns of the local banks. One could be servicing high-income, large lawns of individual homeowners. Others could be niche, where they handle the shrubbery of companies and other companies handle the lawn service. The point is that target markets can, and are, varied from company to company.

Market Segmentation's Role in Marketing

The role of market segmentation in marketing is vital to understanding how your target market will intersect with the actual purchasers of your products.

SEGMENTATION TAKES ON MANY FORMS, BUT THE KEY TYPES OF SEGMENTATION ARE

Geographic Segmentation

The goal here is to divide an overall market into groups based on their location. This means that the segmentation process is specific to certain communities, states, regions, or country (group of countries). Companies look at economic variables and geographic indicators to best position their brand(s) to the most suitable customers for their products.

Demographic Segmentation

With this type of segmentation, the division of an overall market into groups is based on gender and age, income and occupation, education level, household size, stage in the family life cycle, and sexual orientation.

Psychographic Segmentation

Division of a population into groups that have similar attitudes, values, and lifestyles. What influences a person's lifestyle? There are many things that influence you: your family, your job, social activities and interests, and the culture you were raised in.

Product-Related Segmentation

In this area, the process is the division of a population into groups based on their relationships/aspirations to a product. The goal is to segment by benefits sought from the purchase of a product. The focus is on the benefits people expect from using the product. So, what are these 75-year-old men seeking when they buy a brand-new red Z06 Corvette? I'm not really sure, but I'll just say their youth.

So, what's the big deal about segmentation, and why is it done? Marketing strategies must be adjusted to meet the needs of diverse groups of people. In order to meet the needs of these different groups, organizations must produce products that meet these differing needs. Market segmentation involves dissecting the varied needs and wants of different consumer groups and how to satisfy those needs.

So, How Do I Know if My Segmentation Strategy is Effective?

There are clear avenues to being certain that you're on the right track with your market segmentation strategy. To be effective, market segmentation must be measurable and present a significant purchasing power, uncover additional distribution sources, or improve your product position and brand awareness. It must be relevant to the organization. Relevancy means that segmentation is sufficiently large enough for an organization to offer strong profit potential to its shareholders. In addition, effective segmentation always must match an organization's marketing capabilities and core competencies. Marketing professionals must be able to promote and serve the market segment that they are targeting. If the segment that you are targeting isn't a segment whose wants and needs are something you can fulfill, you haven't gained anything.

How Do I Know if Segmentation is Producing Results for My Organization?

When companies segment (remember, this is taking a group of potential consumers and breaking them down into subsets), they are viewing the potential consumers' segments against their company capabilities. They are trying to match the target market that they have segmented and placing their core competencies against this chosen group of people.

Invariably, you will know if your marketing strategy (which involves the segmentation process) has been effective if you are increasing market share, improving top-line sales revenue, improving profitability, expanding your base of customers, or any combination of all of the above.

The key point is that your company's position within the industry or industries where you compete will improve if your segmenting process is matching the propensity of consumers to buy with your company's products. It's really that simple. Not rocket science in any way.

CHAPTER 6 REVIEW

By the end of Chapter 6, you should know the following:

- What is the definition of a target market?
- What are the two main types of target markets?
- Who is Walmart's target market? Target Stores?
- What is the definition of market segmentation?
- What are the different types of market segmentation?
- How do you know if your market segmentation strategy is effective?
- What is important for segmentation results to be effective?

Bibliography

Goudreau, Jenna. 2011. "Wal-Mart's Mom-in-Chief Targets Millennial Mothers." Forbes, January 27. https://www.forbes.com/sites/jennagoudreau/2011/01/27/wal-marts-mom-in-chief-targets-millennial-mothers-advertising-campaign-consumer-supermom-real-women/#6ed7e56a3d7f.

Halzack, Sarah. "Target's New Strategy: We Need More than Just Minivan Moms." The Washington Post. March 04, 2015. Accessed May 24, 2019. https://www.washingtonpost.com/news/business/wp/2015/03/04/targets-new-strategy-we-need-more-than-just-minivan-moms/?noredirect=on&utm_term=.0b3ffbf49f6a.

FIGURE CREDITS

CHAPTER 7

MARKETING RESEARCH AND SALES FORECASTING

Here's the deal: marketing research and sales forecasting are hard. They require dedication and extraordinary commitment to detail. It's the unsung heroes who are always doing the work when others get the reward. Marketing research is very much the unsung hero of the marketing world. The people who work in marketing research are extremely bright and dedicated, pursuing the best information that can be disseminated to the marketing team. This information is important to make informed, concise, organized, and educated decisions about marketing directions. The scope and depth of a marketing campaign an organization puts into practice begins with marketing research, allowing an organization to effectively articulate the competitive landscape within which it competes.

What is the Marketing Research Process?

The marketing research process is ongoing and must be done as organizations develop strategies and product to meet the needs of consumers. So, what does this entail?

Defining the problem, conducting exploratory research, formulating a hypothesis, creating research design, collecting data, and interpreting and presenting the data are all parts of the marketing research process. But at the core of marketing research is data mining, which is a very intensive study to understand your target market(s) and how to ensure that you are satisfying their needs.

Marketing research is at the root of all product development. It is understanding trends of the industry and dissecting the data to develop a plan to have a strategy to maximize an organization's position in the industry where you compete.

Most companies in every industry partake in marketing research. There are some industries that put a large portion of their resources toward marketing research (e.g., consumer packaged goods, fast-moving consumer packaged goods, consumer electronics, food and beverage, automobile).

So, who conducts marketing research? There are many different types of marketing research. Some examples of the types of companies employed to gather, interpret, and report marketing research are listed below:

SYNDICATED SERVICES
Provides standardized data on a periodic basis to its subscribers.

FULL-SERVICE RESEARCH SUPPLIERS
Marketing research organization that offers all aspects of the marketing research process.

LIMITED-SERVICE RESEARCH SUPPLIERS
A company that specializes in a number of activities, such as conducting field interviews or performing data processing, but not sophisticated modeling.

What About Collecting Data?
Within the realm of marketing research, there are basically two types of data that companies focus on to ensure that they are capturing the most accurate industry, consumer insights, and trend reporting for their organization: primary data and secondary data.

FIGURE 7.1. Big Data Image

PRIMARY DATA
Data within the primary collective is extremely detailed, has multiple levels (think drop-down menu), costs a lot of cash to obtain, and provides a more accurate depiction of where your organization stands within the industry where it competes. When you think of primary data, the key component of this research information almost always includes separate companies providing multiple layers of information regarding your brand.

For example, there are companies that are solely involved with certain aspects of data.

TREND REPORTING

Companies here are focused on providing industry information, market share, and where your brand is positioned from a market share perspective. This is very much centered on collecting sell-in data, the units and dollars of product that have been sold to dealers (retailers). Trend reporting is highly specialized and hard to obtain. This is the heart of marketing research.

CONSUMER INSIGHTS

Organizations focused on consumer insights usually have highly qualified clinical/consumer psychologists employed at their company. They are continuously engaged in studying consumer behavior. It's more art than science. This practice also engages consumers where they live—in stores and online. The idea behind consumer insights methodology is to follow consumers and understand their buying habits, purchasing behavior, and redundancy (what they purchase consistently).

SHOPPER MARKETING

Companies engaged in shopper marketing are very much like consumer insight organizations. It's a very blurred line, and even this little industry is confused about what their role is in the consumer's mind. Having worked in the shopper marketing industry, I can tell you shopper marketers always say that the consumer and the shopper are different. This is not always the case. Consider pet food, for example; the consumer and shopper are clearly different. Well, I guess they could be the same in extreme situations (joke intended). Shopper marketing organizations are a fairly new addition to the marketing arsenal, usually subsidiaries of giant parent companies that subsidize their existence. Their only focus is on capturing you, the consumer, while you're in the shopping aisle. These companies also engage in display/corrugate design and marketing messaging to supplement sales revenue. I've never really understood the need for shopper marketing as a separate entity. Companies that have the marketing talent within their ranks should easily be able to provide this smaller incremental revenue with the employees they have on staff.

SECONDARY DATA

The key concept to note between primary and secondary data is that secondary data doesn't cost the user anything, but the data can also be outdated and not relevant to true trends in the market. This data is also normally collected by someone other than the user. Examples of secondary data include censuses, information collected by government departments, organizational records, and data originally collected for other research purposes.

Interpreting and Presenting Marketing Research Data

Companies compile intensive marketing research data that is designed to play a multitude of roles within the organization. Most important, data is king: it keeps us all honest in how we view our current business situation, future business opportunities, and the competition.

Within the current business, we need marketing research to tell us how we are doing within our own company. What is driving this product category to grow where another is lagging behind the industry? Marketing research tells you this. It is imperative that you understand why you are not doing well in certain areas but you're knocking it out of the park in others. What are the reasons? There can be many factors affecting differing businesses that you currently are monitoring. These factors are uncovered by marketing research. Many factors include economic stability of the country, how your product is priced within the market relative to your competition, your sales force capabilities, your company's core competencies, and the general health of the industry where you compete.

Marketing research also helps you develop a business plan for future business opportunities. Research is always a guide, a barometer that allows your senior management to make decisions. These decisions must be made with objective, and not subjective, data. This is where marketing research thrives. To understand whether you should be involved in future business opportunities normally involves delving into a new branch of a category, a totally different category, or an existing category with improved/superior products. Marketing research uncovers how the industry that you're targeting is performing. Do you really want to be involved in an industry that is down 20% versus prior year? There may be a strategic "yes" to that question, but it must be uncovered, which involves reams of industry data.

How about marketing research being used within the competitive environment? Why would this be necessary? You know who your competitors are, right? Not necessarily. You need to understand your competition thoroughly, not just what they are doing today. Marketing research can pinpoint what your competitors are working on today and how their focus may drive a push into a new market. Or research may show that a competitor is storing up cash and has the ability to fight a price war. Would this concern you? Of course it would, as this would put you at a competitive disadvantage on cost.

FIGURE 7.2. Chief Executive Officer Image

CHIEF EXECUTIVE OFFICER

Once marketing research data has been retrieved, reviewed, and weighed against your organization's strengths and weaknesses, the data must be presented. This is normally done through the head person within the research department of your company. They present usually to the "C-suite" of persons at the company—the highest level of officers who make decisions regarding the vision of the company. It's that simple. The marketing research data is drilled down into an executive summary that shows clear, concise data values that determine whether or not a company needs to be competing and at what level within a current or new industry.

Sales Forecasting and its Importance to Business Planning

Sales forecasting is probably one of the most, if not *the* most, redundant processes that sales and marketing professionals engage in. It is imperative to the financial health and wellness of the organization. Why is this?

Sales forecasting keeps you out of trouble from an inventory standpoint. Misjudging inventory needs can have a lasting effect on a company's bottom line. What is the bottom line? It's a company's net income. So, why is this a big deal? Think of it this way. Imagine you own a company that sells floor mats to the automobile industry. The automobile industry is supposed to grow next year, hypothetically, at over 25%. Based upon this data, you increase your sales forecast on all floor mats for all makes and models of cars due to this industry data showing expected growth.

What happens if the market doesn't grow and in fact declines for next year by 10%? What happens to your company's net income? It is severely negatively impacted, isn't it? Why?

HERE'S WHY

- Assuming you expect a +25% growth and the industry declines by -10%, you have a sales forecast miss by 35%.
  Now, assume that the total number of floor mats you supply is normally 1,000,000 units at a cost of $25/unit.
  We've already said that you are going to miss by 35% (expected 25% growth; industry declined by 10%).
  You purchased an additional 250,000 units of floor mats for your accounts, right, because you thought the market was going to grow 25% AND the industry also collapses by 10%, so you lose an additional 100,000 units due to the negative industry performance.
  This means that you've over-purchased on your sales forecast by +350,000 units. Is that a big miss or a big deal to your company? You tell me. This means that your company is going to miss a sales forecast by $8,750,000 in cost dollars—so, yes, it's a huge deal!
  Not only have you lost almost $9,000,000 but you also have to continue to warehouse this inventory, and that gets very expensive. Assume inventory carrying costs are somewhere in the neighborhood of 3% per month per unit (for every unit you have to hold in your inventory, the cost to do so is 3% of the cost of goods of that item); you have another $262,500 of bottom-line profit dollars that you are spending just to hold inventory that you cannot get rid of.
  So, what do you do with this inventory? You have to promote it, which is one of the key marketing principles we've discussed already in this book. You have to mark down the product to entice your accounts to buy the inventory so that you are relieving the inventory carrying costs, as well as moving through the product to make room for new floor mats that must be manufactured as new automobiles are produced with different floor mat specifications.

- I hope this exercise shows you how important the sales function is within a company. Again, it is a redundant process that happens weekly in many companies. You must be correct in forecasting sales into your account base, as this affects inventory control, supply chain, and logistics. In addition, you must also manage the movement of products through the chain: sell through.

By the end of Chapter 7, you should know the following:

- **What is the marketing research process?**
- **Is marketing research an ongoing, continual process or a one-time exercise?**
- **What are some examples of industries that engage in extensive marketing research?**
- **Give examples of companies that conduct marketing research.**
- **What are the differences between primary and secondary data?**
- **What is the goal of interpreting marketing research findings?**
- **To whom is marketing research data presented in the organization?**
- **What is sales forecasting, and why is it important?**

FIGURE CREDITS

RELATIONSHIP MARKETING AND CUSTOMER MANAGEMENT

I debated, quite honestly, on where this chapter should be placed within the body of this work. After a long talk with myself, I finally came to the conclusion that it belonged in the middle of the book. I wanted to build up to why relationships are KEY to your success as a person, business professional, and company. There is NOTHING more important than relationships. They are key to everything you do in life. Forget business for a minute—the key point for relationship marketing is to know that it has ALWAYS existed since the beginning of time, and we're going to dive in and pursue this truth further.

Relationships are Key to Everything You Do in Your Life. Period.

It does not matter whether you're in business, your personal interactions, your family, your marriage, your significant "other," your dog, etc.—if you don't have a good, solid relationship, you will fail. It's just that simple. Do you believe me? I have had relationships with people in

FIGURE 8.1. Babies Hugging

business that I didn't trust because of one reason or another. I've had people tell me, "You don't have a strategic relationship with your account"—they were complete idiots, and I mean that sincerely. I pride myself on building relationships, caring for them, and nurturing them. You must do this in order to be successful in life.

No matter what you do in life, you MUST have trust. You must have trust in other people to know that you are respected, the person or company "has your back," and that you are in this situation together. If you do not have this, you are not going to be successful. If your relationships aren't built around trust, there is absolutely no way that you can have a sustainable business model.

In my career, I have always been honest with my employers, my peers, my accounts, and everyone I have ever come in contact with. I have never been the most vocal person in meetings because I think it's unproductive—you talk when you have something important to say. You take copious notes; you follow up; you are accountable; you do what you say you're going to do. You build respect and trust this way—you build relationships. It's social intelligence—knowing when to speak, when to act, reading body language, and being sensitive to the buyer's needs.

It's insane to me the number of senior managers I've met throughout my career who felt that the more people talked and bullied, the more they were contributing. It's actually funny. In truth, these people are the most insecure people on earth. They are idiots, and they fall hard. I've seen it happen to many people in my career.

Now, on to relationships in marketing—uh, they're important. Did I say that before?

Relationship marketing focuses on long-term partnerships with customers. Does that make sense? Of course, it does! Have you ever had a job and lost credibility with a customer? Whether it was on a golf course or in a clothing store, or wherever? What did that feel like? It hurts, doesn't it? You must always do what you say you're going to do—that is what builds credibility, trust, and a long-standing relationship with customers. There is no other way to build it. It also takes time. You must consistently prove that you will get done what you say you will do.

Transaction-Based Relationships

Do transaction-based relationships exist within businesses? Yes, they do. Transaction-based relationships occur when there are very few interactions between you and a buyer or when very little communication is necessary between the buyer and the seller.

Can you think of any instances in which transaction-based relationships exist?

What about buying a pair of headphones at a store where there is a salesperson versus buying online? There is interaction at the store, and you build somewhat of a rapport with the salesperson who is talking with you. With online sales, the opportunity doesn't exist, so it is always going to be transactional.

FIGURE 8.2. Digital Marketing

According to Hubspot, "Digital marketing is an umbrella term for all of your online marketing efforts." Businesses leverage digital channels, such as Google searches, social media, emails, and websites to connect with current and prospective customers. There are many digital marketing companies that have popped up in recent years. Their goal is the same as any other marketer: to entice you to buy their products. Digital marketing uses very robust digital assets to show off products in their best light, giving potential consumers all angles of a product, specifications of the product, product reviews, etc. In addition, digital marketing tries to uncover the best opportunities to ensure that brands and models show up faster when you search for an item. They use search engine optimization techniques, social media, digital content, display ads, search ads, and various other methods to improve how their brands are positioned. However, even with the breadth of the digital world's reach and success, there is no interaction with the customer face-to-face, and nothing will ever replace strong relationships you build by sitting across from the buyer.

Building Buyer-Seller Relationships

Organizations understand that they must build relationships with customers to grow and expand their businesses. This is the bedrock of any transaction. When a buyer develops a strong, positive feeling within a long-term buyer-seller relationship, it is a benefit for customers and suppliers.

Companies must be very cautious about their relationships with customers. A customer (in this case, a buyer) may switch loyalties if he/she perceives better benefits and pricing from a competing company. You, as the seller, must always be diligent, knowing the market, understanding what the buyer is looking for, and keeping an eye on what your competition is doing.

FIGURE 8.3. Colleagues Fist Bump

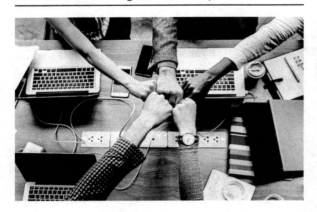

It is easy to become complacent in the buyer-seller relationship, just as it is with any relationship—but you must constantly be evaluating what can be done to better serve the buyer and make yourself invaluable to him/her. You must do this because as soon as you leave a meeting with the buyer, someone is right behind you trying to steal your business (i.e., market share).

So, let's also talk about a phrase that you've all heard, which is "buyers buy from people they like."

Do you believe this? It's absolutely true. If a buyer doesn't trust you or just feels like you're not genuine, he or she will find every excuse in the world to keep from buying from you. It's the truth, so be yourself when meeting with buyers, let them get to know the "real" you, and always do more than expected after the sales call.

So, Why Do Customers Leave?

Customers do leave you for "greener pastures." It happens, just deal with it and go on. There are myriad of reasons that a buyer would not purchase a certain product from your company, and they can be quite extensive. Some of the reasons buyers might not purchase from you is that they are going out of business (severe case, of course); they feel they are not getting the best price for the product type (happens every day); they no longer have a need for the product (they have found a cheaper alternative, or better brand, or stronger feature content); they prefer a newer or competing brand.

Successful companies are cognizant of the signs that a customer is thinking of leaving their brand and have plans in place to ensure that they retain the customer. These contingency plans take on many forms. Sometimes, a customer is looking for an exclusive product, better pricing, more advertising dollars, more attention, better service, broader assortment, etc. The company that quickly realizes the issue(s), puts an effective plan in place, and executes on the plan will usually win the customer over, keeping the customer from engaging with its competitors.

Types of Partnerships

There are several types of partnerships that exist within the business arena. For this reading, we will focus on three of the key partnerships that exist within the buyer-seller relationship. The use of the term "partnership" here is concerned with the interactions between the entities that buy products and those that sell products. For anyone who has been in sales, you know that these relationships (whether you're on the buying side or the selling side) can be tumultuous at times, and extremely rewarding at others. The key point is that there is always going to be some contention as you implement marketing strategies and sell products.

So, let's get started.

WE WILL START WITH BUYER PARTNERSHIPS

Buyer partnerships are ones in which purchases of goods and services are from suppliers, where the buyer trusts all aspects of the product and its ability to satisfy needs. As a buyer, your job is to ensure that you are placing the very best products on the retailer's shelves. This doesn't just include the way the product looks, or the packaging, although these are key factors. In addition to these attributes, a buyer is also looking at the product's feature content versus the competition's, the cost (and ultimately margin), the retail price point (is it competitive), the merchandising funds given by the supplier, the end-of-life strategy (what is the supplier doing to help sell through the balance of the inventory at the end of a program), and much more.

NOW THAT WE KNOW WHAT BUYER PARTNERSHIPS ARE, WHAT ARE SELLER PARTNERSHIPS?

Seller partnerships are the reverse of the buyer role. As the seller, you are immersed in the feature content and all of the additional elements of how the product is viewed from the buyer's perspective. So, in essence, you and the buyer are locked in a mutually beneficial partnership that involves an exchange of goods and services. The difference in the partnership, as a seller, has more to do with the true "salesmanship" of the relationship. A seller, in general, must be very knowledgeable about what he/she is selling. Remember, the buyer is counting on you to know how his/her product fits in your assortment, how the product is differentiated from the competition, and why you should place the product on the shelf. It is your job to convince the buyer to place your product. It's your job to influence his/her decision. You need to be credible, believable, likable, and genuine. Do you see a pattern emerging within the realm of marketing? Business is not hard if you are willing to do the work, focus on the customer (buyer), and fill a need that the buyer has in his/her product assortment. If you can do this consistently, your buyer-seller partnership will flourish and continue for years.

WHAT ABOUT INTERNAL COMPANY PARTNERSHIPS?

Internal partnerships are relationships involving customers within an organization, and they are the foundation of the organization's ability to meet its commitment to external entities. Okay, so that's a mouthful. What does it mean?

To begin to understand internal company partnerships, you need to understand what a company's competencies are and how they operate. Did you know that most companies, whether listed as Fortune 500 or as simple as Joe's Lawn Service, use other services (or companies or people) to provide an element of the business need that they cannot provide on their own? It's true. It happens in most organizations. For example, did you know that "Apple has always had a hard time divorcing itself from Samsung's chipsets and similar products, and that remains true for the iPhone X and its Samsung-made NAND flash memory chip and DRAM chip," according to *TechRadar*, October 2, 2017? The point is that "no man is an island"—companies with internal partnerships have symbiotic relationships where they mutually benefit from any given situation. The thought process is that they can't provide the need on their own, so they must partner with others to provide the need to the customer. Makes sense doesn't it?

CHAPTER 8 REVIEW

By the end of Chapter 8, you should know the following:

- **What is *the* most important thing to build in business *and* in life?**
- **What is a transaction-based business relationship?**
- **What does digital marketing mean?**
- **Why do customers leave?**
- **The difference between buyer and seller partnerships.**
- **How do internal company partnerships work?**

FIGURE CREDITS

Fig. 8.1: Source: https://pixabay.com/en/life-beauty-scene-siblings-brother-862967/.
Fig. 8.2: Source: https://pixabay.com/en/online-marketing-internet-marketing-1246457/.
Fig. 8.3: Source: https://pixabay.com/en/team-team-building-success-computer-3373638/.

CHAPTER 9

PRODUCT STRATEGIES

We have talked a lot about the definition of marketing, how relationships matter, the elements of marketing, target markets, segmentation, reference groups, influencers, etc. However, one of the key principles that business stands upon is that product is king. If you don't have a great product, you don't really have a lot to sell OR talk about. Have you ever heard the phrase "like putting lipstick on a pig?" If your product is weak, your entire strategy is going to be WEAK.

You must have great products that people want to buy. You can't put a successful product strategy together if your product is undesirable. Does that make sense? Of course it does. Okay, so now that we understand that product is king, what do we do to enhance our company's product strategy? What can we do to ensure that our product assortment is maximized within our distribution (channels of trade)?

We Need to First Talk About Our Product Mix

The product mix of a company is an assortment of product lines and individual product models within the different product lines. The product mix is one of the most consistently discussed, consistently modified, and hotly contested areas within a company. If you're not growing, you're

FIGURE 9.1. Red Ratchet Tools

dying; remember that comment? It's true. This is the reason why product mix is such a huge issue with companies. You must get this right. No exceptions. No excuses. No matter what. Does it always work perfectly? Uh, no.

The point is that companies must try to mitigate potential landmines that will keep a product line, product model, etc., from selling. It's a fine line, a balance that is constantly measured within the confines of corporations.

Within the product mix is the product mix depth, which is the total number of product models within a product line a company offers within differing product categories.

The product mix assortment is the total number of total products or models that a company offers. Within a company's product assortment, there are models that provide a lower margin to the retailer and ones that offer consistently higher margins. Why would companies (or suppliers) have different products with different margins that they offer? It all has to do with the feature content of the products and filling the needs of the consumers and the retailers that you sell products to. Think about it: Apple offers several iPhones, right? Are you going to buy the newest iPhone X or are you happy with the iPhone 8? It all depends, right?

Are you willing to pay more for higher capabilities (storage, speed, screen size), or are you good to go with a lesser version? Everyone's needs are different. That's why companies have different models to sell to retailers and ultimately to you and me, the end consumers. Another reason companies (suppliers) offer a varied assortment of models is that they want to ensure they have a product mix that has a blended margin. What does that mean? In its most basic form, a blended margin product mix means that manufacturers are providing consumers and retailers with a choice of products, but also providing lower and higher margin products to retailers. Retailers need lower margin items; these items are products that are sold at much lower prices to consumers. They are also priced lower at retail because they are the entry-level models that retailers depend on to drive foot traffic. These items bring customers into the front door so that you and I will hopefully see that higher featured product and want to buy it versus the lower featured (and lower priced) item. Does that make sense?

What About Product Quality? How Important is it?

Remember what we discussed in this chapter? Product is king, right. Of course, product quality is extremely important. There are instances where you are less concerned about product quality, of course. The instances where this might happen would be when a product is less technology driven. For example, if you're buying kitchen trash bags or fly swatters, you're really not extremely concerned about product quality. However, when you're purchasing a connected TV or smartphone, you are very concerned about product quality, aren't you?

Just ask Samsung how important product quality is.

Samsung is still reeling from their phone batteries igniting while in use. According to an April 16, 2017, article by Jessica Dolcourt on CNET, "the lithium-ion batteries used in mobile phones contain flammable chemicals that are usually separated within the battery structure. And if they touch for any reason? That's when massive overheating and internal fires happen. It turns out, this occurred in both the original and replacement batteries for two totally different reasons."

So, how did Samsung react and handle the situation? Again, from Jessica Dolcourt and CNET's April 16, 2017, article, here's how the company formulated their damage control strategy:

FIGURE 9.2. Samsung Galaxy Note 7

- Samsung recalled the Note 7 and promised to exchange the phone for a new model with a different battery, or give owners a different Galaxy phone, or get a refund.

- Some replacement Note 7s burned up, too.

- Samsung recalled the Note 7, and completely ended production.

- Everyone stopped selling the phone (legally). CNET gave back all review units.

- The FCC and airlines banned the Note 7 from all flights, including hand-carry and checked luggage—even though flight attendants no longer have to point it out at the start of each flight.

- Samsung collected the phone at airport kiosks, sent millions of text messages to Note 7 screens, pushed software to cap battery charge, and cooperated with local carriers to cut service to Note 7 phones.

- Samsung wrote an open letter apologizing for the incident, backed by full-page apology ads.

- Samsung's profits suffered in late 2016; the company estimates that the Note 7 recall will cost $5 billion in all.

- The company announced the causes of battery burnout on both the initial Note 7 run and also on the replacement phones.

- Samsung says it recovered 96 percent of its Note 7 phones back from global customers and 97 percent in the US.

So, what do you think? Did they do a good job of damage control? They handled the situation very well. Unfortunately, it will still probably hasten the retirement of several key people involved. Samsung is a very well-run company, many of whose employees I know and respect immensely.

However, the Galaxy Note 7 debacle still cost them, didn't it? No one knows if the $5 billion figure is accurate; however, think about it: $5 billion of net profit dollars. What would you have to sell to generate a net income of $5 billion? It depends upon what your gross margin percentage is, but let's just say, a lot!

Product quality is extremely important for any organization, large or small. And if you have an issue, you address it immediately, as Samsung executive management did in this case.

And guess what? According to an August 24, 2017, Statista report, "a recent survey conducted by Creative Strategies and SurveyMonkey, as posted by Caroline Cakebread, for businessinsider.com, U.S. consumers, especially current Samsung users, are unfazed by last year's events. More than 80 percent of the respondents who currently own a Samsung phone would definitely or maybe consider buying the Galaxy Note 8."

In fact, the article goes on to say:

> Although most consumers surveyed are skeptical of the new phone, Note 7 owners—i.e., the ones most affected by the recall—appear more than willing to forgive Samsung. Owners of the Samsung's Galaxy Note 7 had the phone taken out of their hands thanks to a worldwide recall. Despite that, they're the consumers most excited about the device's successor.

It's important, always, in business and in your personal life, to deal with issues head on, quickly and decisively. Samsung acted professionally, swiftly, and decisive, always with the end consumer in mind.

Benchmarking Yourself Against the Competition

What is benchmarking, and why is it important when we are talking about product strategies? Benchmarking is measuring quality by comparing your company performance against industry leaders. Think of benchmarking as doing a very thorough evaluation of your company's key abilities, your core competencies, and how they compare to industry leaders. Do you think Procter & Gamble, Johnson & Johnson, Campbell's Soup, Microsoft, Cisco, Sony, and American Airlines perform these evaluations? Of course they do. It's important to always know where you stand against the competitive environment.

Benchmarking involves three main activities: identifying processes that need improvement, comparing your internal processes to industry leaders, and implementing changes for quality improvement.

IDENTIFYING PROCESSES THAT NEED IMPROVEMENT

Most successful companies are continually looking for ways in which they can improve their operations, whether this is involving true operations of the business, sales, businesses they are engaged in, etc. Why do they do this? It's to make sure that they are not missing opportunities or being usurped by the competition. It's important to know what you do well and know what you need improvement on. We do this evaluation in our personal lives, and companies do the same within their organizations. It helps to mitigate risk, lessen surprises, and keep the organization lean and operating efficiently.

COMPARING YOUR INTERNAL PROCESSES TO INDUSTRY LEADERS

Why do companies merge, consolidate, and expand their businesses into additional areas? Most of the time it's because a company is either unable to provide the process, product, or service to their customer; or it's because a competitor has developed an innovation that they need in order to survive. In any event, the important thing to understand is that companies must understand their processes and how they compare to competitors. These processes take many forms and can affect the bottom line severely if not addressed.

IMPLEMENTING CHANGE FOR QUALITY IMPROVEMENT

As you embark upon the benchmarking process, every company will find areas that can be improved upon. It's important to quickly implement an action plan to identify deficient processes and/or practices and assign owners to the implementation initiative. Larger organizations enact these initiatives much more frequently than smaller companies. It's very easy for larger companies to become entangled in layers of management and mired in e-mail and not get much done. Making changes is good for the organization, its employees, and shareholders. This process shows that companies are not shy about the need to fix what is broken, leave alone the areas of operations that are working, and continue to develop long-term planning.

Hardware and Services as Strategic Initiatives

As companies grow and expand their businesses, they are exploring alternative forms of recurring revenue streams. What does that mean? It means that companies in the business community continue to develop new ways to add top line sales revenue-producing entities to their portfolio of businesses.

For example, one company, Xerox, has done an excellent job of selling their expertise, combining services to their hardware sales. Other examples of companies that are heavily involved in selling both hardware and services are Oracle, Microsoft, Cargill, Hewlett Packard, IBM, and British Petroleum, to name a few.

FIGURE 9.3. Xerox Logo

Why would companies involve themselves within the service sector of the business when hardware is their main product that they sell? It's simple. Many organizations are looking to both decrease overhead (the cost of doing business) and expand sales revenue. One way in which they can do this is through the use of their expertise.

Think about it: producing physical product costs a lot of money due to many factors that include tooling, component parts, physical freight/movement of goods (supply chain), and inventory storage (warehousing). To be able to offset the higher overhead costs of the hardware with services is key due to the ability to negate the need for overhead.

With services in most instances, you're selling your expertise, your company's brainpower. This involves helping companies develop new ways to innovate, streamline processes, improve performance of systems, etc. The point is that there is an avenue in the services area to improve sales revenue and decrease overhead as services revenue increases. Companies that are enhancing the services area of their business are generally better off from a fiscal point of view.

The Product Life Cycle

When you embark upon your business career, it doesn't matter whether you will be involved in marketing, supply chain, accounting, finance, information systems, management, or another area of expertise—you will always hear the phrase "product life cycle." Why? Because it's an essential part of the business rhythm of all companies engaging in the marketing and sales of products.

So, what does it mean? Product life cycle is how the product (or product line) is managed from its introduction, sell in, sell through, and end of life.

Let's keep going on this. When companies introduce new products—let's take Apple, for example—they must already have a fairly good idea of how many units of the "new model" they are going to sell. Does that make sense? It's really looking at the many areas of the new introduction and how it will be bombarded by competitive pressures. How does a company know that this is going to happen to the newly introduced product?

HOW DO THEY KNOW THAT?

They know because of past history forecasting of like models (e.g., iPhone 8, iPhone 7, etc.). The new model is different, yes, but as a company, you do know several things that help you determine what to produce for the consumer demand that will be generated. You know how many consumers purchased the previous models, you know how many new customers will be in the market, you know what the average replacement base of consumers will be, and you know what the anticipated, pent-up demand will be for the new feature content on the new model(s) being introduced. You also know your competition well. You know what they are going to be working on, their strengths and weaknesses (remember SWOT?).

With this information, you have a good idea of how many units to produce that will take you from product introduction to the end of the product life. Then you start all over again with the new model introductions that will come after. It's a continuous cycle, and sometimes it happens more than once per year.

Think about that.

In the consumer electronics realm, the personal computer industry has approximately four product life cycles per year (depending upon the brand). That means that companies must produce the product, understand anticipated consumer demand, forecast the demand, build to the forecast, sell the product into your account base (channels of distribution), and plan for reserves to mark down what is left at the end of the product life cycle, and then start all over again—four times per year! That's a tremendous amount of pressure to place on product planning, engineers, marketing, research and development, supply chain, etc.

Why does this happen? Why are there so many product life cycles in the consumer electronics business? The consumer electronics business, by definition, is considered a hypercompetitive industry. According to Wikipedia, "hypercompetition occurs when technologies or offerings are so new that standards and rules are in flux, resulting in competitive advantages and profits resulting from such competitive advantages cannot be sustained." This ain't your Glad trash bag kind of industry; it's serious, it changes quickly, it has many entrants, the margins are very thin, and the innovation is constant.

To expand on innovation further: your innovation is never going to be sufficient enough to outpace the industry, resulting in continual reliance on research and development to produce better-performing products than your competition, better packaging, stronger feature content, etc. It's never-ending and can be a ton of fun! Some of my best friends are the geekiest people you will ever meet and they are crushing it.

CHAPTER 9 REVIEW

By the end of Chapter 9, you should know the following:

- In business and marketing, what is king?
- Why is the product mix of an organization important?
- What is the difference between a product line and a product mix?
- Is product quality important as a strategy initiative?
- Know the Samsung Galaxy Note 7 mobile phone case study.
- What is benchmarking? Why does benchmarking need to happen?
- What is the product life cycle? How does it affect the organization?

Bibliography

Cakebread, Caroline. 2017. "People Who Owned the Galaxy Note 7 Are Excited for the Note 8—Despite Last Year's Battery Debacle." Business Insider, August 24. https://www.businessinsider.sg/samsung-fans-are-ready-for-the-galaxy-note-8-chart-2017-8/.

Dolcourt, Jessica. 2017. "Samsung Galaxy Note 7 Recall: Here's What Happens Now." Cnet, April 16. https://www.cnet.com/news/samsung-galaxy-note-7-return-exchange-faq/.

Wikipedia. n.d. "Hypercompetition." https://en.wikipedia.org/wiki/Hypercompetition.

FIGURE CREDITS

MANAGING AND DEVELOPING BRANDS

Why do companies use brands? What is their purpose? How do companies decide on what they will call themselves? What is the process to determine brand logos and names? It's a fascinating study to understand this. Sometimes brands are thought up in the most obscure ways. Brands are the heartbeat of a company. They are the driving force of a company. Employees want to protect the brand they work for, enhance it, and get more and more people to buy it. I've never been prouder than to have been a Sony employee. I worked for the brightest people (the first generation of managers in the 1990s) in the world, and I mean that. The company loved the employees; they fought for them; and they respected them. I think a lot of the demise of Sony happened due to the way people were treated after the founding fathers started to retire and new blood came into the company.

Let's talk about managing and developing brands further.

Let's take the Apple logo. Although the logo has evolved from the first design created back in 1976, most people recognize that iconic brand on the back of your MacBook Pro. The logo was not the result of thinking about the biblical story of Adam and Eve or the great Sir Isaac Newton and the concept of gravity.

According to an October 7, 2011, CNN report by Holden Frith, "Unraveling the Tale Behind the Apple Logo" and a quote from Rob Janoff, the man asked by Steve Jobs to draw up the logo: "he's hazy about how he settled on the simple outline of an apple, the reason for the bite is crystal clear: it's there for scale, he says, so that a small Apple logo still looks like an apple and not a cherry." You would think that the energy behind the creation of the meaning behind brands takes lots of time and energy and input from a lot of talented people. Sometimes that true, and a lot of the time it just isn't. As the article by Frith goes on to say, and in Rob Janoff's own words, the iconic logo was the brainchild of one person, Janoff:

Figure 10.1. Apple Logo

> Sadly, the evidence now points in a more prosaic direction. In a 2009 interview with **CreativeBits**, Rob Janoff, the man who drew the logo, reflected on the theories about his work. He dismisses Sir Isaac or the Bible as source material and, while he says he is charmed by the links with the Turing story, he says he was unaware of them at the time.
>
> "I'm afraid it didn't have a thing to do with it," he said. "It's a wonderful urban legend."
>
> Janoff says that he received no specific brief from Steve Jobs, and although he's hazy about how he settled on the simple outline of an apple, the reason for the bite is crystal clear: it's there for scale, he says, so that a small Apple logo still looks like an apple and not a cherry.

That's how brands get decided in many instances. It's that simple. No huge deep, underlying message (although some do have deep meaning). No huge brief to get started on the "creative juices" to get the brand developed (Steve Jobs gave Rob Janoff no brief, no direction). In most instances, brands are simple, easy-to-remember logos or names that help you identify a company and its products.

What is a Brand?

A brand is any name, term, symbol, design, or some combination of these to identify a company. Brands identify and differentiate products from one company to another.

FIGURES 10.2A,B,C Different Logos—BMW, Toyota, Univ of Tennessee

FIGURE 10.3. Starbucks Outdoor Café Area

Think about just the clothes that you're wearing and what is in your backpack right now. You have a myriad of brands that are on your possession all the time. You have shoes, socks, underwear, pants, undershirt, shirt, possibly a hat, watch or wristband, glasses, sunglasses, makeup, cologne/perfume—and that's just what's attached to you. Now think about what's in your backpack.

See where I'm going with this? You are a walking billboard for companies. And they know it.

Do different brands mean different things to you? What do you think of when you review a brand like Louis Vuitton versus Coach, or BMW versus Mercedes? Are there big differences that come to mind? Maybe not as stark as thinking about a Toyota Prius versus a Tesla. They are basically the same type of automobile (i.e., electric assist), but in your mind, the brand and price/value relationship is vastly different, isn't it?

What about the university that you are attending? Do they have a brand? Yes, they do. You're probably wearing it or have the university brand somewhere in your closet.

Branding proliferates everywhere globally. We love brands, and that will never change. Companies that understand their consumer, understand where their products fit and take advantage of this, win.

Why is Starbucks successful? After all, it's only coffee. Oh no, my friend. According to a March 1, 2018, article in Spoon University, there are five reasons why millennials love Starbucks and pay higher prices for their product.

CONCEPT

Starbucks was the first to realize that people like to gather, to meet. And they like to meet in a place that provides a "customer-centric culture." It's true, isn't it? I'm not a millennial, but I like Starbucks. It's a fun, inviting place to be. I don't have to feel like I'm rushed or that I'm in a library setting. All around me I see people working and enjoying the concept.

LOCATION

Starbucks provides a great place where people can meet. As the article says, and as we know, retail is all about "location, location, location."

AMBIENCE

I think we all like the look and feel of Starbucks. I like its comfortable feel and that most people are enjoying the time that they spend within the building.

PRICE

This is one area that has both good and bad connotations to it. According to Spoon University, "Coffee is an essential. You can't live without it. It's either you love it or you hate it." I believe that is the brilliance of Starbucks. Their coffee costs a lot of money, yet they fill most Starbucks locations each and every morning because they get everything else right.

SERVICE

A question that the Spoon University article raises is "Have you ever come across rude Starbucks staff? I surely have not. They're fast, efficient, friendly, energetic, and they call your names out correctly, but there's only one thing, they can't spell it."

Is this your experience? It's been mine. They never get my name right. I spell my name Jon and it's always spelled John when I get my grande café mocha, but do I care? No. The staff is always very fun and enjoyable to deal with.

Do you see a pattern emerging here? It's amazing when you have a great concept, great location, the atmosphere is inviting, and the service is impeccable. When these things are right, guess what? You'll pay a higher price for the product. That's the entire point.

I.   How Do Customers Become Brand Loyal?

I think we've answered part of this question in our last section. How do some brands create such fierce brand loyalty in customers? That's THE question that most companies are trying to obtain the "secret sauce" to understand.

Let's begin another way: have you ever purchased a product that you really desired and then had a horrible experience with it? I have. I will not name the PC maker, but I purchased a PC from a well-known manufacturer. A manufacturer that has a tremendous amount of market share. I had an issue with one of the keys sticking on the keyboard, so I took it in to get it repaired; it was then sent off to the manufacturer for repair. I was out of commission with my PC for eight days. It came back, and when I hit the "return" key, the PC would shut off. Okay, I'm done. I want my money back. No three strikes with me. I can't deal with product that doesn't work. Doesn't matter what it is, who it is, or the reputation they have.

So, one of the key ways that customers become brand loyal begins with the product. The product must be great, satisfy a need, and be dependable. That's not too much to ask, is it? No.

And when product functionality is compromised, everything is compromised, especially my loyalty to the brand. Yours is, too. You may still add the brand to your consideration set, but it fades in its exclusivity to your purchase decision.

It's about product, but also your experience. Are you having consistent, positive interactions with the product AND the

FIGURE 10.4. Ford Explorer

company? If the answer is "yes" to both, then you are most likely either very aware of the brand or brand loyal.

Your environment also affects your brand preference and how loyal you are to a particular brand.

My father never bought anything other than a Ford pickup. I really love the exterior look of the GMC product, but I could never bring myself to purchase a GMC pickup. Why? Because I would feel like I was disloyal to my father. Do you have similar brands that you've been "conditioned" to own? It's amazing how your personal experience, family, and friends influence your brand preferences.

II. Dissecting Brand Names

We've talked about brands and how consumers become brand loyal, but let's really dig into brands and understand the reasoning behind them. What made the company choose the brand name (or icon), and is the brand working? There are brands that you can't live without; which ones are they, and why do you feel that way? It's very personal and something that only you know the answer to.

Companies want to know why you chose their brand over others. And they want to make sure that they are positioning their brands to you in a way that identifies their company. So, in essence, a company chooses their brand in a way (in most cases) by how it wants to be positioned (thought of) in your mind.

FIGURE 10.5. Haagen-Dazs Store

For example, when you think of Haagen-Dazs, what do you think of? A very high-end Swedish or Danish company with a few specialized workers laboring over the perfect blend of ice cream mixes? You would be wrong: Haagen-Dazs is straight from the streets of the Bronx, New York. It's true. Pillsbury acquired the brand in 1983, and today it's owned by General Mills. Haagen-Dazs is part of a multinational conglomerate and is just one of hundreds of brands under the General Mills umbrella. Does that surprise you?

Every brand has a story, a meaning, and a purpose. Some of these brand names are extremely simple. Take Ford Motors, Inc., for example. How did it get its name? Henry Ford owned the company and he put his name on the Model A at the very start, and the rest is history. For other branding, the reason for the name takes on deep meaning—lots of thought, and it is part of an overall mission statement and can imply the need to push social causes.

Many times, organizations also use sub-brands. Microsoft owns Xbox. The Microsoft name is not seen on any of the Xbox packaging. Sony owns PlayStation. It goes on and on. Branding happens also within a company's product lines; Sony Trinitron TVs, for example, or Sony XBR.

How about Apple TV? The sub-branding is very widely used with companies to set themselves apart from the competition and focus intently on pushing a brand within a brand.

III. What About Brand Extensions?

Many companies want to diversify their portfolio of products and extend their brands into entirely different products, separate from their main brands. What does this mean? As a company starts producing products that it is known for and they continue to grow and improve their market share within an industry, they seek to ensure that they will continue to expand their business by expanding their brand into new areas. Does this always work? No. However, there are instances where brand extensions have been wildly successful.

Nautica is known for apparel, right? Did you know that Nautica also makes watches? How about Harley Davidson—you know the iconic name for huge, cruising motorcycles. However, they also produce perfume, wine coolers, and sunglasses. In 1959, Mattel introduced its first Barbie doll. Barbie had blond hair, blue eyes, and a figure that in all respects was not representative of the average woman's true body shape. According to a January 28, 2016, article by Shan Li in the *Los Angeles Times*, "somewhere along the way, moms began to think that her impossibly thin body, out-of-proportion bust, and sky-high stiletto pumps sent the wrong message to their daughters in an increasingly image-conscious world."

IV. What About Brand Licensing? How Does That Work?

Brand licensing expands an organization's exposure in the marketplace. Licensing your brand allows you to retain ownership of the brand while another company produces the collateral and marketing campaigns to push the brand to higher levels in the minds of the end consumers.

What is it, exactly? According to Wikipedia, brand licensing "is a process of creating and managing contracts between the owner of a brand and a company or individual who wants to use the brand in association with a product, for an agreed period of time, within an agreed territory."

Brand licensing allows the brand owner to receive royalties from the company using the brand. Think of brand licensing as renting the brand for a period of time. You are the owner, always, yet allowing other companies to promote and sell the brand. In a licensing agreement, the owner of the brand name is the licensor and the company wanting to license the brand is called the licensee.

FIGURE 10.6. Polaroid

One company that comes to mind is Polaroid. What a great brand name. Well, it used to be, right? Polaroid was founded by Edwin Land in 1937 and at its peak employed 21,000 people in 1978. In fact, Polaroid had such a huge impact on the consumers' mind-share that we used to say, "let me take a Polaroid of that" rather than "let me take a photograph." It's unbelievable brand awareness. Much like Kleenex. Most people today will say "can you hand me a Kleenex" versus "can you hand me a tissue?"

The decline of Polaroid came in the early 1990s when they did not garner much market share as the digital world invaded it. Polaroid never recovered, laid off thousands of workers, and became a shell of itself, eventually filing for bankruptcy in 2001. Having worked for Polaroid, I have firsthand knowledge of the company, its people, how the company faltered, and the final demise of the company and its pitiful existence now as an owned license. It really is a sad story for an iconic brand that should be still living on today.

Today, there really is no Polaroid company; it's a license. There are factories that have the Polaroid brand licensed and are trying to sell their televisions, instant cameras, and various other upstart product categories this latent company is trying to produce.

CHAPTER 10 REVIEW

By the end of Chapter 10, you should know the following:

- What is the definition of a brand?
- Know the Starbucks case study.
- How do customers become "brand loyal?"
- What does brand positioning mean, and how does this happen?
- What is a brand extension? Do you understand examples of brand extensions?
- What is the definition of the term "brand licensing?"

Bibliography

Frith, Holden. 2011. "Unraveling the Tale Behind the Apple Logo." CNN, October 6. https://www.cnn.com/2011/10/06/opinion/apple-logo/index.html.

Li, Shan. 2016. "Barbie Breaks the Mold with Ethnically Diverse Dolls." *Los Angeles Times*, January 28. https://www.latimes.com/business/la-fi-mattel-barbie-20160128-story.html.

Ooi, Annie. n.d. "How and Why Starbucks Is So Successful." Spoon University. https://spoonuniversity.com/lifestyle/how-and-why-starbucks-has-been-so-successful.

Wikipedia. n.d. "Brand Licensing." https://en.wikipedia.org/wiki/Brand_licensing.

FIGURE CREDITS

CHAPTER 11

SUPPLY CHAIN: THE MOVEMENT OF PRODUCTS

Supply Chain is an Integral Part of Marketing and Critical to a Marketing Plan/Program's Success.

The physical movement of goods from manufacturers to end consumers is part of the logistics and supply chain. This is the way in which manufacturers move products to you. The supply chain process is complicated with thousands of moving parts (figuratively and literally). There is a myriad of upstream and downstream elements to the process that must be clearly understood, constantly monitored, and continually tweaked to perfection. It is a monstrous undertaking the larger a corporation is and requires tremendous attention to detail, hourly communication, and collaboration between raw materials producers, component manufacturers, canneries, bottlers, suppliers, and retailers.

Another term for this is distribution, the process of how goods move through the supply chain system. Remember, distribution in marketing means where you are selling your products. It's the classes of trade where you are distributing your products. Distribution in supply chain terminology means how a company is moving products across the country and globe to retailers, wholesalers, and the end consumer.

FIGURE 11.1. Supply Chain

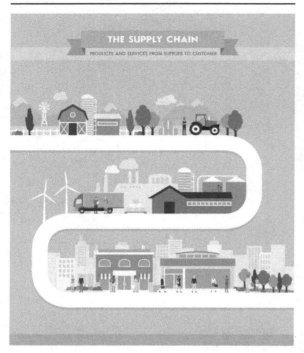

What Demonstrates an Effective Supply Chain System?

An effective, properly run supply chain management system (or process) is when product is received when it is supposed to be received. It is a very simple concept with extremely complicated processes. The elements of the supply chain involve the control of the activities of purchasing, processing, and delivery of goods. As products move through the supply chain, there are multiple "touch points" that need to happen in order for the process to work flawlessly. Unsurprisingly, it is never flawless. Supply chain and logistics are extremely difficult due to availability issues with manufacturers, raw materials suppliers, component suppliers, freight delivery issues, communication errors, etc.

The most effective supply chain management develops when there is a regular cadence between all of the "owners" upstream and downstream. What does this mean?

FIGURE 11.2. Suply Chain Network

Within every supply chain system, all parties must understand the upstream process. Upstream is the beginning of the process, for lack of a better term. It's where the product ideas begin: raw materials are set up to be sent, and the product is manufactured. As you move downstream, you begin to deal with areas such as product quality, testing, packaging, warehousing, staging, transportation appointments, carrier movement, and ultimately delivery to the end consumer.

This all sounds so mundane and not a part of marketing. Is this important in marketing? Is it a vital part of marketing? Without an effective supply chain process, you and I would not have our needs satisfied; we would walk into a store and the product wouldn't be there. That would be disappointing, wouldn't it? And it would possibly change your view toward the brand that disappointed you with no stock available.

How Important is the Distribution/Supply Chain to an Organization?

It's vital. The distribution (supply chain) function accounts for a large portion of a company's total marketing costs because the cost of moving goods, freight, and inventory carrying costs are extremely expensive. The larger the organization, the more important the supply chain and logistics arena becomes.

Walmart is a company that is very efficient at every step of the chain. They consistently develop new ways to cut costs out of the system and continue to provide EDLP (Everyday Low Price) to their consumers. One way to do this is to continue to streamline the process. Walmart arguably has one of the best supply chain systems in the world, according to an article in supplychaindigital.com submitted by James Henderson on June 20, 2018:

FIGURE 11.3. Walmart

Ft. Wayne—Circa June 2018: Walmart Tractor Trailer. Walmart is boosting its Internet and e-commerce presence to keep up with competitors.

> The report by Kantar Retail named Walmart, Kroger and Costco as the top three retailers with the best supply chain management. The report said: "The top retailers on Supply Chain Management remained largely consistent compared to last year, representing a wide range of channels." Walmart once again retained its #1 position, gaining about 80% of manufacturer mentions—a testament to its continued dedication and expediency in this area. "Kroger and Costco maintained their #2 and #3 ranks, followed by Publix, which rose one rank to #4. Target came in at #5, having swapped positions with Publix."

What sets them apart is that they continually try to improve on a model that is already very well run. In addition to ensuring that they have their processes in place, they put a lot of pressure on their supplier network to improve as well. One of these areas that they have recently implemented is OTIF (On Time, In Full). The mandate is that suppliers will have product to Walmart within a very short window, and the expectation is that 100% of the purchase order is delivered. OTIF has shortened the receiving window for suppliers, placing a greater degree of pressure on their supply chain metrics to ensure that they adhere to improving Walmart's out-of-stock position within any product category.

The key for Walmart and any retailer or manufacturer is to try and identify activities that do not add value for customers. Product not on shelves is one of the worst retail sins that can be committed, and all retailers (along with their manufacturer partners) try and avoid this at all cost. It is a major detriment to everyone involved in the supply chain.

Let's Talk About the Physical Distribution of Goods

The physical distribution system for most companies contains the following elements:

CUSTOMER SERVICE

You must be able to handle customers with care. Genuine care. Companies that are able to handle customer issues quickly and efficiently are most likely going to keep those customers. Within customer service, there are various issues that arise. Many of these deal with return of merchandise, online issues, payment issues, and the like.

TRANSPORTATION

Moving goods across the country and the world takes a monumental effort. The way companies handle transportation needs varies from one brand to the next. Some large retail companies like Walmart, Target, Costco, and Sam's Club have their own fleet of trucks to move products from their distribution centers to their stores/clubs. The same goes with very large manufacturers like Samsung, Procter & Gamble, etc. Their distribution and transportation needs are so great that it makes sense to have their own fleet of trucks. Smaller manufacturers or licensees will many times employ 3PL (third-party logistics) companies to help with the physical movement of products. They have the relationships with the retailers and have vendor agreements already established, making it much easier to transact.

INVENTORY CONTROL

Controlling inventory costs is important to the financial health of any organization. Inventory control means the forecasting, planning, replenishing, ordering, warehousing, and monitoring of inventory flow. Inventory is the physical product that is sitting in the warehouse waiting to be shipped out to customers. One of the most important areas of inventory control is forecasting and planning. As we have said before in this book, if you get inventory needs wrong (high or low), it always has a negative impact on your business, as you will either have too much inventory (therefore needing to promote it to deplete it) or you have too little (and angry customers waiting for product).

FIGURE 11.4. Inventory Management

PROTECTIVE PACKAGING AND MATERIALS HANDLING

Companies spend millions of dollars on packaging every year. This is necessary to keep costs low but also to minimize damage due to mishandling and dropping, as well as sustainability pressure. These factors have given rise to a focus on improvements in packaging and biodegradable packaging. Most experts in the field of packaging would tell you that there hasn't been much headway here, although some companies are trying to push for more awareness to the need for sustainable packaging and the need to decrease waste.

By the end of Chapter 11, you should know the following:

- What is the definition of supply chain?
- What is another name for supply chain?
- How do you know when you have an effective supply chain process?
- What is the importance of supply chain to an organization?
- What are physical distribution elements and the importance of each?

Bibliography

Henderson, James. 2018. "Walmart Recognised for Best Supply Chain Management." Supply Chain Digital, June 20. https://www.supplychaindigital.com/scm/walmart-recognised-best-supply-chain-mangement.

FIGURE CREDITS

RETAILERS, MERCHANDISING, AND PRICING

What Exactly is Retailing, and What Does it Really Mean?

Retailing involves any activities that focus on selling merchandise to the end consumer, and retailers come in many forms today. There are many books that have been written on retailing: best practices, mistakes made, resurgences, and consistent growth. There are many different retail classes of trade (also called channels) that include mass merchants, national superstores, warehouse clubs, regional retailers, buying groups, one-store operations, convenience, and e-tailers. We won't go into all of the different retail channels, but suffice it to say there is a fair amount of retailing operations, each one providing a different customer experience for you and me, the end consumers.

Retailers create the space and merchandising where customers can interact with their goods and services. Even if that "place" is online, which has seen explosive growth over the past few years, with this trend expecting to continue.

FIGURE 12.1. Merchandising

Okay, So What's this Thing Called Merchandising?

Merchandising is nothing more than how you see products sitting on the shelves when you walk into Target, Best Buy, Walmart, 7-Eleven, or any other retailer to purchase an item(s). It's the way in which a retailer's products are displayed/presented to the consumer. Merchandising is at the heart of marketing and a fundamental part of how products are viewed (your perception of the brand).

FIGURE 12.2. Cosmetics

Merchandising is the number of models, pricing, packaging, and product mix of a brand on a retailer's shelf. Have you ever walked into Walmart and wondered why TVs are at the back of the store? It's to draw you back into the store.

FIGURE 12.3. Walmart

What about the color on the end caps, the aisles? Bright colors invite you, keep you walking further into the store. Is this intentional? Of course it is. What Walmart wants you to do (and, by the way, all retailers) is to purchase more than one item. They want every customer walking into the store to have a multi-item basket when they leave the store. That's how they win. They want your disposable income to be left at their store, not the competitor's.

There are many books written just about this subject—it's fascinating, half art, half science. There is a reason for the why and how manufacturers package their products, price them, and which models are sold to which retailers. It's a very detailed part of the marketing process.

The Merchandising Mix and its Role in Marketing

Let's first define what the merchandising mix is. It is the totality of the product offerings of a company to its customer base. A merchandising mix is terminology used more in retailing than it is for manufacturing. However, manufacturers can use this term interchangeably with product mix (as we've discussed in a previous chapter). This includes a company's differing product lines, designed to target different classes of trade. The needs and preferences of its target market are varied. The key here is to remember that manufacturers produce the product. They are the starting point. Every year (sometimes more than once per year, depending on the product category), manufacturers and retailers have product planning meetings, line reviews, and merchandising meetings to ensure that manufacturers are developing products their retailer base wants. There are retailers that are more focused on the very best price that a retailer can provide its consumers (think mass merchants). And there are retailers that want these entry-level products but are more focused on higher-end goods that offer higher prices (and hopefully higher margins). These retailers are predominantly regional retailers and national superstores.

The competitive environment is also a concern of every manufacturer and retailer when they put together their merchandising mix. For example, Walmart doesn't want to compete with the exact product (merchandising) mix that Target has on their selling floor. Why? Because there is always the possibility of retail conflict, pricing conflicts that impede negotiations and drive a wedge between the manufacturer and the retailer. Why the manufacturer? Because many times the retailer will try and persuade the manufacturer not to sell another retailer the same model. It happens all the time, which is why many manufacturers will provide a differentiated product line or product model(s) for different retailers.

The overall profitability of each product line and category is another consideration for manufacturers and retailers. In most instances, the lower the feature content, the lower the price point of the product and the lower the margin is to the retailer. The profitability of a product line or category must be "blended" into the entire profit and loss statement of the strategic business unit of the company to understand the impact of selling different products to differing retailers.

What Does the Battle for Shelf Space Mean, and Does it Really Exist?

Companies are competing for the disposable income of every consumer who enters a retail location or website. Best Buy wants to relieve you of your disposable income so that you cannot use those dollars when you walk into Walmart or Target or Costco. Do you believe that? It's true.

The companies that succeed have products that are consistently selling and are at the correct price point that meet the price/value relationship in the minds of consumers. As a manufacturer, your goal in most instances is to continue to expand the number of products you have on a retailer's shelf. Your goal is to grow your sales revenue while keeping competitors' products off the retailer's shelves. The battle for shelf space is CONSTANT—the competition never stops!

The proliferation of new products and variations on existing ones have increased the competition for shelf space. Models and SKUs (Stock Keeping Unit) are ever evolving with technology and product improvements.

Let's Talk About Pricing

What about pricing? Is the pricing of products considered a strategy? Pricing is by far one of the most effective strategies companies employ in efforts to attract consumers to purchase their products. Pricing has always had a tremendous effect on consumer perceptions of your brand.

Over the past years, price wars have emerged, and price has become an even more focal point of retailers' agendas. Think about Black Friday: Black Friday is more and more crucial every year for retailers. The retailers' Black Friday ads are a closely guarded secret. However, every year there continue to be "leaks" of the ads early. This means that the Black Friday advertisements that retailers are going to release just prior to Black Friday are "leaked" early to the

FIGURE 12.4. Pricing Strategy

public. Consumers want to know what is coming. It's the buildup, the anticipation of what is going to be that new breakthrough price on a Samsung TV or Apple iPad, iPhone, etc.

In times of intensive competition, it is getting even more important for retailers to focus on profitable, and successful pricing strategies as retailers/e-tailers are in an environment of complex circumstances: broad assortments, intense competition (most recently from online companies), fickle consumers, and an ever changing retail environment.

Because of these reasons, retailers should define a clear framework for their pricing strategy. We will talk about pricing as it relates to strategy more thoroughly in the last chapter.

CHAPTER 12 REVIEW

By the end of Chapter 12, you should know the following:

- What is the definition of retailing?
- What are the different classes of trade that are generally accepted by retail outlets?
- What is merchandising, and why is it important in marketing?
- What is the marketing mix?
- How important is the battle for shelf space to manufacturers?
- How much does pricing affect the competitive landscape?

FIGURE CREDITS

Fig. 12.1: Copyright © Janine (CC by 2.0) at https://commons.wikimedia.org/wiki/File:Drinks.jpg.
Fig. 12.2: Copyright © 2015 Depositphotos/mandritoiu.
Fig. 12.3: Copyright © 2014 Depositphotos/wolterke.
Fig. 12.4: Copyright © 2016 Depositphotos/garagestock.

CHAPTER 13

ADVERTISING, COMMUNICATIONS, AND PUBLIC RELATIONS

First, Let's Talk About What These Media are Not

Advertising, communications, and public relations are NOT interpersonal selling. You cannot replace the face-to-face selling process to build relationships between yourself and the customer. The influence of personal selling and advertising, etc., are completely different.

The process of physical selling involves a more intimate, personal contact from individual to individual. Personal selling is a presentation conducted on a face-to-face basis with a buyer. This is the oldest form of sales interaction.

What About Advertising? What is it?

Advertising seeks to develop initial demand for a good, service, organization, person, place, idea, or cause. Advertising messages can take many forms and are designed to spur the audience to purchase products, instill goodwill, and/or enhance a company's brand through positive brand awareness.

There are many different strategies companies employ with advertising campaigns, designed to spark action for different reasons.

What are Some Examples of Different Advertising Venues?

There are many different advertising campaign message strategies. Some are persuasive advertising, informative advertising, institutional advertising, product advertising, and comparative advertising, to name a few. In addition, there are also various types of advertising venues, such as billboard advertising, broadcast campaigns, print campaigns, and online advertising (display ads, search, etc.).

Where else do you see advertising that is happening more and more as the telecom industry expands? Smartphones. Smartphones have increased the number of purchases consumers have transacted via their mobile phones.

What is the Goal of Advertising?

Advertising needs to educate consumers about a specific product, product introduction, or the brand itself. The advertising message needs to improve the perception of the brand while "selling" the need to purchase the product. Extremely effective advertising will produce consumers loyal to your brand.

The bottom line of advertising messages is to increase sales or improve a company's brand image.

FIGURE 13.1. Isaiah Mustafa

What themes do companies most often use when they are utilizing advertising? The main themes used by companies to capture your attention and spur you to act are fear, sex, humor, emotion, and urgency of time (to purchase).

Think about it: you see an ADT commercial that shows a nice home in a nice neighborhood and the narrator of the piece is playing on the viewer's fear of home invasion. What about sex? You see it every day—just pick up a magazine, turn on the television, get on the Internet. There is an ad out there that is focused on telling you how great the latest eyeliner will enlarge your eyes (the sexual implication is that the eyeliner makes your eyes more alluring), or the provocative commercials where a beautiful young woman is slowly eating yogurt off of a spoon (the connection trying to be made is if you eat this particular yogurt, you will somehow morph into this beautiful young lady). Humor is everywhere in advertising; this needs no explanation. What about emotions, pulling at your heartstrings? The goal is to get you to donate to their cause, and they tug at your wallet through emotional connection to their cause.

What About the Communications/Public Relations Process?

Corporate communications and public relations are completely different from advertising. The biggest difference between advertising and communications/public relations is that advertising is messages that are delivered through paid media. Public relations and corporate communications are the company's directives to have direct communications with their consumers, letting them know what is going on with the latest company strategy, product, or goodwill initiative.

Communications is vital to building and maintaining the corporate image of a company, and most Fortune 500 companies have corporate communications departments. Public relations is used in many circumstances but mainly to promote the goodwill of a company, damage control, and to convey key corporate messages to employees.

Do you think Samsung's corporate communications and PR departments were on high alert when the Galaxy Note 7 started to catch fire due to a faulty battery? Of course they were. The immediate response was to do damage control (ensuring that they met the problem head on). And they handled it marvelously, with one of their telecommunications managers going on television to apologize for the issue. In a video message to Samsung consumers, as reported by Tim Hardwick, September 16, 2016, for MacRumors, a senior official for Samsung Electronics America, Telecommunications Division, Tim Baxter, relayed to consumers:

> "We apologise, especially to those of you who were personally affected by this. To those of you who love the Note, the most loyal customers in our Samsung family, we appreciate your passion and your patience. We take seriously our responsibility to address your concerns about safety. And we work every day to earn back your trust, through a number of unprecedented actions and with the extraordinary support of our carrier partners, suppliers, and the United States Consumer Productions Safety Commission."

That message to Samsung consumers was classily done, timely, and no excuses were made—just an exact process for how Samsung was handling the situation and ensuring their customer base would not suffer from their mistake. Very well done, indeed.

FIGURE 13.2. Public Relations

CHAPTER 13 REVIEW

By the end of Chapter 13, you should know the following:

- What is the difference between advertising and interpersonal selling?
- What is the definition of advertising?
- What are the different ways in which consumers see advertising?
- Explain the goals of advertising.

- What are the themes used by marketers when they advertise to consumers?
- Explain the difference between advertising and communications/public relations.

Bibliography

Hardwick, Tim. 2016. "Samsung Addresses Note 7 Customer Concerns in Video Message Apology." MacRumors, September 16. https://www.macrumors.com/2016/09/16/samsung-addresses-note-7-customers-in-video/.

FIGURE CREDITS

PRICING AND PRICING CONCEPTS EXPLAINED

Pricing and its Influence in Marketing

Pricing is generally determined utilizing various methods, but all involve three key areas: supply and demand, cost, and price. When you affect any of these variables, the others will change. No matter the method, pricing of products and services is a key determinant of the success or failure of a company's marketing strategy.

In a September 16, 2016, article by Eric Loveday of Inside EVs, Elon Musk congratulated employees on an excellent third quarter but also said "it is absolutely vital that we adhere to the no negotiation and no discount policy that has been true since we first started taking orders ten years ago." The same article goes on to say "Musk … grateful, yet at the same time disgusted with employees for apparently discounting cars without an order from the top."

In some companies, negotiating on price is not optional. Let me ask you a question: do you believe since that article was written that there haven't been more negotiations with consumers walking into a Tesla new car showroom? I'd bet money that there have been. The point is that in the Tesla organization, pricing is strictly set and nonnegotiable. It is an anomaly and certainly not the norm.

FIGURE 14.1. Tesla Automobile

How Do Companies Use Pricing to Help Achieve Their Marketing Goals?

Pricing can be used in several ways to help determine a company's future. Developing a pricing strategy involves understanding the direction of the company and adjusting pricing to achieve goals.

Companies either have market share (sales) goals or profitability goals, and they fluctuate from year to year. What do you think Samsung's Telecommunications Division goals were after the Samsung Galaxy Note 7 debacle? Sales or profit? I was not in any of those meetings, but I have been in meetings at Samsung in other divisions, and I would venture to say their goal was market share protection—sales revenue!

FIGURE 14.2. Samsung Phone on Fire

When Would a Company Use Pricing in their Marketing Strategy, and Why?

This pricing thing appears complicated, doesn't it? It can be, but it's really just a function of the marketing strategy organizations employ. Companies use pricing in their marketing strategies each and every day. Pricing is without doubt one of the most heavily regulated parts of the marketing process. It's vital to an organization's ability to develop strong cash flow, establish a brand through price/value relationship, and to enable the organization to produce profitability for its shareholders.

If the goal is to improve market share, a company would most likely lower pricing to gain a stronger market share foothold, thus improving sales, and by default earn more of the market. In addition, lower pricing could also open up additional classes of trade or distribution points to companies wanting to grow their business.

A company that needs to show profitability to investors would most likely increase pricing (all things being equal) to help improve the bottom line profitability. However, improving profitability is much harder than gaining market share based upon price. Why? Because when companies are focused on profitability, in most cases they need to raise prices. There are other ways to improve profitability. You can reduce your headcount, capital expenditures, etc. Those are accounting functions. In marketing, the focus on profitability normally revolves around pushing strong innovation. You must give consumers a reason to purchase higher-priced products. They aren't going to do this "just because." You must innovate, creating products that consumers want to pay more for, thereby improving your position in the market with credibility and also improving the bottom line with additional profit margin.

Does this always work? No, there is a fine line between increasing pricing and decreasing sales to the point where the profitability isn't improved due to lack of demand for products. This happens a lot with companies. Every company starts the year with their annual initiatives to improve their position within the market where they compete. In most companies, there are two key initiatives that fluctuate from year to year. The fluctuation normally involves whether the company is focused on profitability for the given year or sales revenue. They are not equal, and one is not dependent upon the other. If you are selling more products, that does not equate to being more profitable, and vice versa.

WHAT IS THE ROBINSON-PATMAN ACT?

The Robinson-Patman Act, in its most basic definition, is federal legislation that prohibits anti-competitive pricing. A seller charging competing buyers different prices for the same item may be in violation. The Robinson-Patman Act prohibits selling at an unreasonably low price to eliminate competition. This act was initially inspired to protect small grocery store operations targeted by large grocery store chains that were lowering pricing so severely that companies were being put out of business because they could not compete.

According to the American Bar Association, the Robinson-Patman Act of 1936 is a United States federal law that prohibits anticompetitive practices by producers, specifically price discrimination. It was designed to protect small retail shops against competition from chain stores by fixing a minimum price for retail products. The specific definition as stated by the American Bar Association:

> "... prohibits certain forms of price discrimination in sales transactions. 15 U.S.C. § 13 et seq. Congress enacted the RPA in 1936 to protect small businesses from larger businesses using their size advantages to extract more favorable prices and terms from small businesses. While the Sherman and Clayton Acts are very broad statutes with open-ended language—the practical meaning of which is brought to life only through court interpretation—the RPA, on the other hand, contains very specific language. Thus, the starting point in any RPA analysis should always be the language and structure of the statute."

The law grew out of practices in which chain stores were allowed to purchase goods at lower prices than other retailers. An amendment to the Clayton Antitrust Act, it prevented

FIGURE 14.3 Crowd Company Community People Concept

unfair price discrimination for the first time, by requiring that the seller offer the same price terms to customers at a given level of trade. The act provided for criminal penalties but contained a specific exemption for "cooperative associations."

What is a "Co-Op" or "Buying Group?"

In a retailing sense, a co-op, or cooperative, is an organization which combines economies of scale on behalf of its members to receive discounts from manufacturers for goods and services. Co-ops are generally made up of companies that, by themselves, do not have the purchasing power that would be afforded by being a member of a larger co-op group.

Co-ops help each member of the group to compete based upon being able to purchase products and services at a much better cost than could have been done on an individual basis.

CHAPTER 14 REVIEW

By the end of Chapter 14, you should know the following:

- Describe pricing and its effectiveness on market share growth versus profitability.
- How do companies use pricing in their marketing strategies?
- What is the Robinson-Patman Act?
- What is the definition of a co-operative, or co-op?

Bibliography

Loveday, Eric. 2016. "Elon Musk Issues Mass Email to Tesla Employees." Inside EVs, September 29. https://insideevs.com/elon-musk-issues-mass-email-tesla-employees-congrats-q3-push-stop-selling-new-cars-discount/.

FIGURE CREDITS

CHAPTER 15

DEVELOPING A MARKETING BUDGET

How to Get Started with Your Marketing Budget

The first thing to decide on with regard to a marketing budget is to understand what you're trying to do. The marketing plan is always first; then you set the budget. Sound simple? Your marketing budget will take some time to collaborate with your colleagues on best course of action to take in order to achieve desired results, but certainly won't be as hard as, say, the federal budget.

WHAT ARE YOU TRYING TO DO?

- Are you introducing a new product/technology to the market?
- Are you trying to introduce a new line of an existing product category?
- Are you trying to influence industry leaders?
- Are you developing products to compete with already existing products within the industry?

These are some of the key questions that will help guide you with your budget. These budgetary plans are crucial to understand how much money you will need to set aside for the

FIGURE 15.1. Image of Federal Budget

marketing campaign. And in most companies, marketing budgets are a percentage of sales revenue. So, the obvious next question is "what is the appropriate percentage of sales revenue to budget?" The answer is "it depends." As a company, there is not a set budget percentage; however, there are always limitations to the marketing budget, just as there are limitations to every initiative that companies employ within their annual planning process.

What Elements of The Marketing Plan are Included in The Budget?

In simple terms: everything.

FIGURE 15.2. Marketing Plan

Think of the marketing budget just as you would think about your home budget. You wouldn't want to forget any key items or events for your home budget. The same holds true for your company's marketing budget. A marketing budget keeps you on track and lets everyone in the process know how you're progressing at every stage of the plan. A marketing budget is also very much like an account ledger: you need to know every line item that is involved in the process.

A simple marketing budget needs to provide:

- Goals and objectives of the marketing campaign—your goals and objectives need to be clearly stated. These keep you on track and everyone moving in the same direction for the marketing campaign.

- Where you are positioned within the industry—if you hold very low market share, you need to know where best to spend the available dollars to grow share. How do you achieve this? Where is the best opportunity for growth, and how do you focus those marketing budget dollars to get maximum return on your investment?

- Which media will be utilized during the campaign—television (broadcast) is expensive; print is less expensive, but the growth of social media opens up a tremendous amount of potential to effectively reach your audience with less expense. There are, however, times when broadcast is necessary, and normally, the larger the company, the more dollars will be spent here.

- Estimate of costs associated with each medium—the costs of the different media you're utilizing to reach your audience vary. They vary by market size, audience targeted, time/frequency of message conveyed, etc. For example, television advertising/production will be less in Davenport, Iowa, than in Dallas, Texas.

- Time frame for each of the budgetary items—you need to understand how long the campaign will run, item line costs for each element, and what exactly will be the focus for each element. Most important, how will each element (medium) point back to the main message(s) of the marketing campaign, so there is a theme to the campaign?

- Total estimated cost for all items—this is always done in ledger form, itemizing and developing a running time line of the total costs associated with the total program.

- How each of the elements of the campaign will be measured—if each of the budgetary items cannot be measured as to their success, then they should not be employed or be considered in the process of the marketing campaign. You must be able to present the success (failure) of the campaign to senior management. If you are not sure how an element of the plan can be measured, again, don't use it. There are a lot of companies trying to figure out better algorithms with social media to measure success. As social media continues to grow, the ability to understand if your marketing campaign is making an impact will be more important. You need to understand how your customers are finding you.

How Do You Reach Your Current and Potential Customers Within a Budget?

First of all, you should KNOW your current customers and have a somewhat cogent direction you need to take; otherwise, you wouldn't be spending dollars on a marketing plan to grow your business. There is at least a base of business that you've developed, allowing you

FIGURE 15.3 Customers Shaking Hands

to continue to build upon your customer base. How you employ elements of the marketing budget to "talk" to your customers is important.

So, let's talk about the different avenues you can pursue to continue to preserve your core business and spark growth. It costs less to keep the customers you have, so this area will focus mainly on attracting new customers.

CURRENT CUSTOMERS

- Stay in touch with current customers—keep face time with them. That is the key.
- Build and maintain a strong relationship with your current customers. Sounds so simple, but companies mess this up a lot.
- When there is an issue of any kind, fix it quickly. Never hide from a problem that your current customers have, or they won't be your customers for long. Once again, relationships are EVERYTHING. Without trust, there is nothing.
- Allocate a very small amount of your marketing spend (budget) to your current base of customers.
- Ensure that you have some reserves that are available to take care of sell-through issues, inventory issues, and things of this nature.
- Remember, with current customers, you're not trying to "sell" to them—you are trying to maintain your relationship with them.

POTENTIAL CUSTOMERS

- This is where you are spending the larger portion of the marketing budget.
- Knowing your target audience is the first key to understanding where you're spending your dollars.
- What is the nature of your business? What industry do you "play" in, compete in?
- Who are your competitors, and how are they reaching their customers?
- What percentage of your business is dot com? Is it growing; should it be growing?
- What can you do to enhance the dot com potential?
- How are you working within your organization, or outside of it, to build robust content on the Internet?
- Do broadcast (TV) dollars make sense within your industry? Unless you're a multinational conglomerate organization, it may not be the best allocation of funds (see Super Bowl spends for dot com).
- Your focus needs to be diving in deep to know where your customers are and reaching them with compelling marketing messages that spark a conversation.

Never Think of a Marketing Budget as a Cost—It is an Investment

Early in my career at Sony (where I cut my teeth), I was under the impression that marketing was a big cost drain on the company. It wasn't until I had the opportunity to learn from great leaders in the company that marketing is an investment. It's a very important investment in your company's growth. Even the most innovative technology has to have a voice, to be heard, to be understood. These are all key points to understanding that you, as a company, must be able to articulate the key messages surrounding your products. Investing in marketing budgets/campaigns allows you to reach your customers and tell them, in differing media, why they should purchase your brand/products over the competition.

FIGURE 15.4. Investment—Piggy Bank

As marketing has continued to evolve over the years, the importance of being able to utilize a marketing budget to provide performance results is ever increasing. Every part of the marketing budget plan must show the spend and the expected return on the spend.

This is crucial today as more sales are being conducted via the Internet. In addition, how the elements of the marketing budget connect are also important. The ability to show senior management how the elements connect to one singular message, the expected lift to sales revenue, and the cost associated with the lift in sales is imperative.

A Marketing Budget is a Tool in Your Toolbox

To use a car mechanic's analogy, imagine trying to work on a car engine without the appropriate tools. You wouldn't get very far (trust me, I've had experience with this). When you start out with no tools, the wrong tools, or you do not know how to use the tools, the effectiveness of the repair lessens.

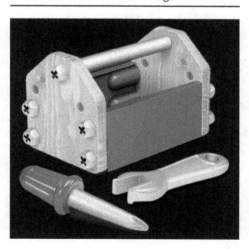

FIGURE 15.5. Toolbox Image

It's the same with the marketing budget. If you utilize all of the stages of the process of setting a marketing budget (as listed above), you will understand that the budget is just one of the tools you have at your disposal to creating a very effective marketing campaign, one that is targeting the appropriate audience, at the right time, with the right media, and within the budget you've determined will provide the greatest return on investment.

By the end of Chapter 15, you should know the following:

- What should you consider when you are putting together your marketing budget?

- What are the elements that a marketing budget needs to provide in order to show a return on the investment?

- What is important in reaching your current and potential customers with your marketing campaign?

- The realization that the marketing campaign (and therefore your marketing budget) is an investment, not a cost to the company.

- Is a marketing budget one of the tools within your toolbox to be an effective marketer?

FIGURE CREDITS

SOCIAL MEDIA AND CONTENT—HOW IMPORTANT ARE THEY?

By far, one of the most important technological achievements of the last 20 years—if not THE most important—is the complete consumer access to the Internet and the transaction speed with which we all can research and educate ourselves on virtually anything. The social media and content available to consumers is reshaping the world as we know it. The lovechild of the World Wide Web is social media, which comes in many forms, including blogs, forums, business networks, photo-sharing platforms, social gaming, microblogs, chat apps, and last but not least, social networks.

Okay, So Who Uses Social Media, and How Do They Use it?

Who uses social media? Everyone with access to the Internet and a smart device to view it on.

Okay, a quick history lesson on smartphones. Did you know that the smartphone wasn't invented until 1992? Even then, the smartphone at that time wasn't very "smart." As mentioned before, I "grew up" in the consumer electronics/telecommunications space; therefore I remember the painful transition from the first introductions of "smart phones" to where we are today, and baby, we've come a long way.

FIGURE 16.1. Smartphone Image

The smartphone didn't become mainstream until 2007. And by smartphone, we define it as a device that allows for software to be installed on it. This was first made available when Apple introduced their Apple stores and provided this service to customers. Imagine that—we have only known a true smartphone with Internet and installation capabilities since 2007. The speed with which technology moves is amazing, and the businesses that have been spawned from this technology are equally as mind boggling.

How Large is Social Media, and Why Do I Care?

According to Statista, the power of social networking is such that the number of worldwide users is expected to reach some 3.02 billion monthly active social media users by 2021, around a third of Earth's entire population. An estimated 750 million of these users in 2022 are expected to be from China alone and approximately a third of a billion from India. The region with the highest number of social media networks is the United States, where around 70 percent of the population has at least one social network account. As of 2017, 81% of the United States population had a social networking profile. Today, consumers' preoccupation with their smartphones is a "thing"—we are all constantly checking social media sites, purchasing, informing, updating, integrating, downloading, and sharing all types of data and images with our coworkers and friends.

FIGURE 16.2 Friends on Smartphone

So, What are the Downsides of Social Media?

There are many downsides of social media, but the overarching fact is that the benefits far outweigh the detriments to having your brand on social media platforms. If you've ever visited Facebook, Twitter, YouTube, Instagram, etc., you have seen the power of social media and the weight that many of these connection sites wield.

FIGURE 16.3. Social Media Mix

Okay, so the positives outweigh the negatives of these platforms, but what should owners of brands/marketers be leery of when out there on social media with their brands? There are a lot of "landmines" that can negatively affect an e-tailer's position online. Here are a few that I consider to be quite detrimental:

9-FEET-TALL-AND-FULL-OF-MUSCLES-SYNDROME

Have you ever heard that term when describing someone that is online and displays a very aggressive style but in person is much more subdued? This happens with regard to opinions about products online all the time. Companies are fallible, they can make mistakes. However, in most instances, companies want to rectify an issue with an online consumer as quickly as possible. Many consumers do not have enough patience to wait for the resolution and send scathing reviews about the company, customer service, the product, etc., even if it's untrue. It happens every day to companies, and it is very hard to overcome negative reviews.

NO FACE TIME WITH THE CUSTOMER

One of the best ways to understand your customer is to be in front of him or her often. That is the best way to understand body language, build relationships, and get subtle (and sometimes not so subtle) hints that there may be an issue that needs to be addressed. The online experience takes this out of the equation, and so the transaction between the company and customer is more transactional and not strategic.

INFLUENCERS' NEGATIVE EXPERIENCE CAN HAVE A DRAMATIC EFFECT

There are influencers in your life who affect what you purchase, when you purchase, and how you purchase goods and services. When an influencer has a negative experience and talks about it on social media, the effect can be widespread and have damaging consequences to the company. When there are connected groups of people in social media, this becomes exacerbated because there may be more than one influencer with negative feedback about a company, its products, or its services.

SOME PRODUCTS ARE HARD TO SELL ONLINE

Can you think of products that you would buy online? Of course you can. Now think about products that you would not consider purchasing online. How about a car? According to the February 2017 issue of *Automotive News*, "nearly 10 percent of all vehicle transactions will be online by 2019." What about clothing, furniture, large appliances, art, makeup, mattresses? Some people would, some wouldn't, but the bottom line is these products are hard to sell. They are all part of individual preferences and need consumers to "touch, feel, smell" the products—its individuality of the experience. The good news: companies are getting better at producing much more robust content to help to sell the items online and showing consumers how best to match a product's size and attributes to their liking.

FIGURE 16.4. Clothing

RETAIL CONFLICT IS MORE PRONOUNCED ONLINE

Okay, so what does that mean? For the vast majority of retailers, there is an online component to their business, as we've already stated. Because of this, the pricing that one retailer has in the marketplace (i.e., manufacturer's suggested retail price, or MSRP) might negatively affect the profitability of another retailer. It is more pronounced online because online there are many more competitors that the retailers must compete with versus brick and mortar.

Best Buy carries a Samsung 55" television and retails the product online at $699. (Let's call it the ABC model.) Walmart carries the exact same Samsung 55" television. However, for whatever reason, Walmart feels that to be competitive within their market(s), they need to drop the retail price of the Samsung ABC model from $699 to $599. What does this do to Best Buy? Can Best Buy keep the same SKU (remember, SKU means stock keeping unit) at $699? The answer is no. Why? Because the lower retail pricing means that Best Buy will sell fewer units than Walmart because their pricing is $100 higher than Walmart. In order for Best Buy to compete and ensure that their unit volume remains acceptable, they must in most instances change their MSRP to $599. In addition, when Best Buy reacts to the market pricing that Walmart has initiated, their margin on this item will fall dramatically. Many times, the retailer will meet with the manufacturer and request that the manufacturer compensate them for the "margin hit." In other words, they (the retailer) ask the manufacturer for a lower cost on that item to maintain their margin to keep competitive.

How Important is Online Content?

Online content is the lifeblood toward being successful with a product or not. As a marketer, you need to understand that you have an obligation to your online customers to provide them with the most robust content available. Okay, so what exactly does that mean?

By any industry statistics and trends reports, the undeniable growth of online sales is growing at a substantial double-digit rate year over year. This growth, has, and will, continue at this pace for the foreseeable future. Therefore, it is prudent that your products are presented in the very best way possible over the Internet.

When transacting with most retailers today, a large percentage will have a dot com component of their product/marketing strategy. The dot com portion of their business is extremely important to all retailers and e-tailers. As such, you, as a marketer, have the obligation to supply the highest-quality images, key marketing messages about the product, and as many 360-degree views of your product as possible.

FIGURE 16.5. Online Content

Think of online content as your sales resource for the products that you place onto an e-tailer's website. Every manufacturer is trying to secure the best possible placement and "click" rates for their products. The more information that you can provide the purchaser, the better opportunity you will have of selling your product online versus your competitors'. In general, the better the descriptors, images (product and lifestyle application), zoom capability, and multiple views, the higher the sales rate will be for your products. Remember, as a marketer, you want to be as clear as possible about the features, benefits, and limitations of the product you've placed online.

Now that seems strange to talk about the limitations of your product, right? Actually, no. The reason you want to be crystal clear about what need your product satisfies and what its limitations are is to minimize returned merchandise. Returns, as we have mentioned, have a large negative effect on a company's bottom-line profitability. In addition, we've talked about the damage negative reviews online can have to a company's image. Ensuring that your product descriptions, images, and key features are correctly represented will minimize negative feedback from disgruntled consumers. Makes sense, right? Companies must constantly look for ways in which to take costs out of the business, and minimizing returns is one way in which to do so.

Most companies that are Fortune 500 and even smaller have dedicated merchandising teams devoted solely to the buying and maintenance of their company's online experience for consumers. In many instances, there is a completely separate staff of replenishment, planning, and operations personnel that handle the dot com side of the business.

CHAPTER 16 REVIEW

By the end of Chapter 16, you should know the following:

- Who uses social media, and how do they use it?
- How large is social media by country?
- What are the downsides of social media?
- Understand the Best Buy example of social media retail conflicts and how this affects a manufacturer's pricing strategy.
- Why is online content so important to a manufacturer that places its product on the Internet?
- Understand the reasoning why the features/benefits of your product(s) must be clearly stated on an e-tailer's website.

Bibliography

Lareau, Jamie. 2017. "Online Car Sales Could Soon Be on Fast Track." *Automotive News*, February 6. https://www.autonews.com/article/20170206/RETAIL06/302069928/online-car-sales-could-soon-be-on-fast-track.

"Social Media & User-Generated Content." 2019. Statista, April 17. https://www.statista.com/markets/424/topic/540/social-media-user-generated-content/.

FIGURE CREDITS

Fig. 16.1: Source: https://pixabay.com/en/agenda-screen-social-phone-1928419/.
Fig. 16.2: Source: https://pixabay.com/en/pokemon-pokemongo-friends-school-1548194/.
Fig. 16.3: Copyright © Blogtrepreneur (CC by 2.0) at https://commons.wikimedia.org/wiki/

File:Social_Media_Mix_3D_Icons_-_Mix_-1_(28011015990).jpg.
Fig. 16.4: Source: https://commons.wikimedia.org/wiki/File:Clothing_organized_at_home_(Unsplash).jpg.
Fig. 16.5: Source: https://pixabay.com/photos/internet-content-portal-search-315132/.

CPSIA information can be obtained
at www.ICGtesting.com
Printed in the USA
BVHW050004100920
588455BV00003B/141